THE SOCIETY OF TRUTH

LEO

A translation of *La Società della Verità*, Leo

To my best friend.

TABLE OF CONTENTS

I

PRINCIPLES

THE INDIVIDUAL

Nosce te ipsum

Life is the totality of individuals. The Individual is a living being composed of body and spirit. The body is the living material entity that shows conditions or performs actions resulting from its genetic heritage, reflexes, thought, and will. The spirit is the unique, non-replicable, thought-originating entity endowed with will and consciousness of self (Subject) and the environment (Object). Between the spirit's act of will and execution by the body, a set of coordinating and memory functions is conceived: the mind.

Regardless of the spirit's material or immaterial nature, it is understood to coincide with the Individual proper: the *ego* or *individual-individual*. If one were to clone a human individual's body, they would produce a body with the same genetic makeup as the former. The same would not be true for the spirit, since at least consciousness and will, conditioned by each individual's experiences, would not be identical. The difference in personality between monozygotic twins, i.e. twins endowed with the same genetic makeup, proves it and, in fact, appearing from the earliest years of life, it shows that experiences are not the discriminating factor.

The primary difference between a human and an animal (or plant) is the prevalence of spirit over body. Man acts primarily upon thought, animals upon instinct (a "mixture" of genetic fac-

3

tors and elementary thought), plants upon their physical and chemical structure (or *phenotype*, i.e. the expression of the genetic makeup). The evolution of Life can be conceived as the gradual transition from matter without thought (inanimate matter) to thought without matter (pure spirit).

Religions and some philosophies argue for the eternity of the spirit, in which case evolution would be the process happening between (1) the contact between matter and pure spirit and their subsequent separation (if matter is eternal), or (2) the creation of matter by pure spirit and its destruction by pure spirit (if matter is temporary).

Evidence of the coexistence of body and spirit is found in the conflicts between them. Physical impulses arousing sexual attraction towards individuals other than one's partner collide with the spiritual feeling of love and loyalty. The need to kill other living beings for the sustenance of the body clashes with compassion.

Earth being the only place to harbor Life, in a Universe containing an estimated number of stars in the tens of sextillions (10,000,000,000,000,000,000,000), in the observable Universe alone, is at least unlikely. Every living being in the Universe, regardless of the proportion of its bodily and spiritual components, is an Individual.

THE UNIVERSE

Individuals act in one or more *universes*. A universe is a set of entities endowed with characters and laws common to the whole. An entity is something or someone that *is*, exists (etymologically, it derives from the Latin present participle of the verb *to be*).

The universe that Man commonly perceives through the physical senses, made of space, time, mass, and energy, is herein called *Universe 1*. The individual's body belongs to Universe 1. The spirit and its will and awareness, if immaterial and therefore not measurable in Universe 1, belong to another universe here named *Universe 0*. Possibly all spirits belong to Universe 0, or each spirit has its own Universe 0, in which case it would share common experiences with other spirits (*communication*) in shared universes of variable duration: Universe 1 would be one of these.

Inanimate space, time, mass, and energy exhibit totally inertial behavior: their change is merely the result of previous events in succession, dating back to a *First Event*, assuming Universe 1 has a finite origin in time, with no variations nor exceptions. The only non-inertial (and therefore unpredictable) changes to be observed are originated by living beings' acts of will unless causality between the First Event and an individual's entire complex thought at the present time is proved. Hence the beliefs that the First Event was caused by an act of will.

By observing high-speed motion phenomena, it has been seemingly discovered that the relation between space and speed is nonlinear: as speed increases, space would compress and time would slow down from the perspective of the moving entity. More or less surprisingly, such a circumstance could greatly facilitate the conquest of Universe 1 by living beings and it would allow the *communication* of virtually unchanged messages between mutually remote points of Universe 1.

Understanding the origin and nature of Universe 1 is the goal of Object Research.

THE PURPOSE

Any *activity* conducted without a purpose is inconclusive and *ends*. A civilization without purpose decays and becomes extinct. A purpose motivates and aligns individual and collective efforts.

Living beings share the *instinctual* purpose to survive, which keeps them alive. It is the most basic purpose, bordering on paradox: the very purpose of not ending. It is an essential trait of Life, which would otherwise be an instantaneous rather than lasting phenomenon. It is an indeterminate purpose, in that it is achieved temporarily at each present moment of survival, but renewed indefinitely for each successive minimal future time unit and therefore never definitively accomplished.

The idea that Life is an end in itself does not seem to be agreeable to Man, who has always set alternative individual or collective purposes, more or less related to survival: soul salvation, Heaven, Nirvana, the eternity of the spirit, pleasure, money, power, glory, peace, the conquest of the Universe, family, happiness, knowledge, fame, justice, art, aesthetics, competence, and so on. The discrepancy between *rational* and instinctual purpose is a further example of the conflict between spirit and body.

The series of famous artists who died prematurely after celebrity and the longevity of philosophers and scientists thirsty for knowledge show the relationship between purpose and individual cessation and exemplify the influence of rational purpose on the attainment of the organic purpose.

Living beings collectively, as well as humankind, lack a consciously and generally accepted common rational purpose. Groups of individuals have historically established partial purposes, often finding in others' purpose a reason for hostility. Known living species other than Man have not even progressed to such a degree of superiority of spirit over body as to be capable of formulating a common rational purpose, so that such a task would still fall to most evolved species.

Establishing a purpose for the entire living society enlists every group and individual in one team. Each individual, in the simplest of their functions, contributes to the overall effort toward achieving the shared purpose. Each individual, when sufficiently self-aware, takes pride in their contribution, is motivated to accomplish their duty, and wants the purpose to be achieved.

Article 4, paragraph 2, of the Constitution of the Italian Republic states:

> Every citizen has the duty, according to personal potential and individual choice, to perform an activity or a function that contributes to the material or spiritual progress of society.

The Purpose of the Society of Truth is to achieve the highest degree of wellbeing for each individual (subject). This is measured in terms of Happiness, Ability, Knowledge, and Freedom, not in terms of material conditions (object), which may be an instrument, not a goal. Purpose measures Progress and regression in terms of approaching and receding from its accomplishment. Progress is gradual and its speed is dictated by the means available.

The highest conceivable degree of wellbeing is a potential state of divinity: being everything, with total Happiness, Ability, Knowledge, and Freedom. It is the complete predominance of spirit over matter. Strictly speaking, the activity pursuing the Purpose will end upon its achievement, thus ending Life as the coexistence of spirit and body.

Society is a *tool* for accomplishing the Purpose. It is a conceptual framework for organizing individual efforts towards the realization of personal potential.

The Purpose is achieved through the attainment and application of Knowledge, in two senses: Knowledge of the Individual (the Subject) and Knowledge of the Universe (the Object).

Formal science has made relatively large strides in the past three centuries, but it has clearly not yet penetrated the core of the object nor the subject. It still clashes with the concept of infinity of the Universe: in space, as absence of boundaries, and in time, as absence of causality. Even the Big Bang theory, describing the Universe's supposed first *cause*, assumes a pre-existing energy supply. The causality issue also appears in the realm of the subject: the origin of Life is unknown.

In the Society of Truth, Knowledge of the Subject and Knowledge of the Object are employed to improve individuals' condition, not to subdue them.

SOCIETY

Society is understood as a system based on *cooperation* and *division of functions* for organizing individuals and groups. It is the conceptual result of a very large number of express or implied agreements between individuals (the so-called *social contract*). Society is meant to facilitate the achievement of the Purpose and it is to end thereafter.

Cooperation aligns and sums individuals' efforts toward the achievement of the Purpose. For a hundred children, a tug-of-war against an Olympic weightlifting champion would be a piece of cake. When considering that the human population numbers nearly eight billion, one can grasp its immense potential in a state of cooperation.

Division of functions contributes to the efficiency of activities directly or indirectly pursuing the Purpose, as everyone invests their resources into learning specific skills to produce *professional* results. With the current educational tools, teaching an individual all professions and trades would require an enormous use of resources and produce an amateur, if they were expected to join the workforce by the age of 30. Functions are not imposed on individuals, they are acquired according to aptitude and will.

Present and past societies have exemplified possible deficiencies in the values of division of functions and cooperation to the detriment of individuals. A society implementing a high division of functions, without cooperation, will end up with individuals and groups fighting each other and regarding their fellow man as a threat. A society that focuses much on cooperation, but little on division of functions, is unprepared, inefficient, and disorganized.

Solidarity is a universal spiritual value that facilitates the function of Society and will survive its termination.

TRUTH

The Society of Truth is the society of living beings founded on Truth. In a community that shares only truth, interpersonal relationships are simple and the economic system is efficient. Trust is the market's backbone: it maximizes the volume and speed of the exchange of goods, thus ensuring the best allocation of resources needed to pursue the Purpose. A market dominated by information symmetry among its players is efficient and balanced.

The first obstacle to the realization of a truth-based world is the inability to *identify* truth. Some doctrines advocate the thesis that truth does not exist and individual observers' perception produces a number of relative "truths". Today's journalism is opportunistically steeped in the worst relativism, and the result is sadly obvious.

In fact, whether someone *observes* an event or not does not change the fact that the event occurred, nor the manner in which it occurred. The factual truth is one, and its correct identification comes through the accurate definition of the event and its circumstances. When available means are insufficient to determine the truth, one should not indulge in the lazy expedient of choosing among possible "truths" and should accept the absence of certainty at that given time.

The second obstacle is the inability to face truth. Here is the realm of taboo. Sometimes truth is painful, but if one does not look at it, their knowledge will be limited. Actions based on that deficient knowledge will be unsuccessful or harmful. Reluctance to face truth can be psychologically defeated by considering that whether or not one is aware of a state of affairs does not change the fact that it exists and affects the individual's life.

The ability to face truth is a graded capacity, differing from individual to individual according to character, education, and experiences. The information system adopted throughout history by most societies and organizations, in which most unpleasant truths have been "reserved" for small groups (police, rulers, priests, confessors, and so on), is based on this fact. A society, in its Progress, increases individuals' ability to deal with truth, so that ever more truth becomes available for all.

The third obstacle to truth is the selfish desire to limit others' knowledge. Information asymmetry in the market favors one party to the detriment of the other. Knowledge is power, and individuals with little awareness of their nature and the social Purpose may want it all for themselves. The Society of Truth is marked by transparency and educates members about the Purpose and the value of individual contribution.

The fourth obstacle, on closer inspection a corollary of the second, is the condemnation of truth. A person confessing misconduct in the name of truth or by virtue of conscience (not out of contingent convenience or necessity) should not be reproached. They are evidently aware of their mistake, without anyone having to point it out to them. Blaming the person would be giving them worse treatment than that granted to those who have committed the same action without being discovered. Once the individual has restored the situation prior to the conduct or repaired any damage caused by it, they should be socially rehabilitated. For serious or repeated crimes, a reformative system should still be implemented.

All other basic principles of the Society of Truth descend from Truth.

FREEDOM

The truth will set you free

Freedom is a cardinal principle of the Society of Truth. Freedom is the power to self-determine one's being and one's material or immaterial acts. Over the course of time, Freedom has been conceived in many forms: freedom from physical restraint (the person of the individual shall not be subjected to detention or other personal restrictions but in the cases provided for by law — Article 13 of the Italian Constitution), freedom of thought, freedom of expression, freedom of communication, freedom of movement, freedom of assembly, freedom of association, freedom of religion, health freedom ("[n]o one may be obliged to undergo any health treatment except under the provisions of the law" — Article 32, paragraph 2, of the Italian Constitution), freedom of education, and so on. These variations of Freedom only describe Freedom within specific areas of human life and in no way represent limits to the general definition of Freedom. The power to self-determine one's immaterial being and acts — understood as thought and will — is not subject to any limits. The power to self-determine one's material acts — understood as any action that is the *direct* and *immediate* cause of a perceivable effect in the material world — is subject to the sole limit of not harming others, i.e. it is subject to the condition that such acts do not diminish others' freedom, unless they constitute legit defense of one's Freedom. Thus, one is not "free" to appropriate another's property without their consent, and one is *free* to stop those attempting theft of their possessions. All possible cases in this regard are exhaustively regulated by national laws.

The freedoms enumerated above pertain to the individual and the groups in which they participate. Nations enjoy typical freedoms too. It is a principle of international law that peoples have the right to self-determination (Article 1, paragraph 2, of the Charter of the United Nations), i.e. the freedom to choose their political system (internal self-determination) and freedom from foreign domination (external self-determination), and it belongs to every people regardless of whether they constitute a state or not.

Knowing one's freedoms as an individual, group, or nation and the factors that threaten them, as well as reacting to any attempt to compress them, is indispensable for their preservation and expansion.

The opposite of freedom is *slavery*, i.e. unconditional subjection to the will of others. Between slavery and absolute freedom there are a number of intermediate stages and advancement through these, for all individuals, represents a society's Progress.

RESPONSIBILITY

In order to preserve and expand one's Freedom, it is necessary for each individual to take Responsibility for knowing and acting. Responsibility can be defined as the ability to regard an object, action, or idea as one's *own*, and normally act accordingly (English speakers also express this concept by the term *ownership*). The antipode of Responsibility is *extraneousness*. Responsibility, after Truth, is the most critical factor for the fate of a nation. Thomas Jefferson wrote:

> If a nation expects to be ignorant and free, in a state of civilisation, it expects what never was and never will be. The functionaries of every government have propensities to command at will the liberty and property of their constituents. There is no safe deposit for these but with the people themselves; nor can they be safe with them without information. Where the press is free and every man able to read, all is safe.

The Constitutions of civilized nations stipulate that *sovereignty* belongs to *the people*. The same Constitutions have established organs (the state in a narrow sense) charged with representing the will expressed by the majority of the population and acting in accordance with it. The right of sovereignty, in order to be preserved in an indirect democracy system, implies the

Responsibility on the part of the individual to keep themselves aware of the state organs' work and of the facts pertaining to the *res publica*, as well as to react to attempts to compress such right.

On the other hand, a "democracy" can be set up in such a way as to *deresponsibilize* the individual, either by mistake or intentionally. A constitutional system that, formally or *de facto*, limits the ways of intervention by the individual in the public sphere represents an attempt to deresponsibilize. When educating a child or worker to responsibility, one gives them instructions and entrusts them with gradually more complex tasks, until they are competent, independent, and *responsible*. In contrast, the devilishly perfect method for making an individual irresponsible is to deprive them of information and functions in the community: the individual feels alien to it, does not perceive it as their own, and does not care about it.

When a state makes minimal or no use of referenda, is not transparent about its political and financial management, uses language incomprehensible to the average person, or reduces democratic pluralism to a sterile two-party system, the voter becomes a *spectator*. Unless this mechanism is promptly responded to, over time the individual becomes completely alienated from politics and regresses to subjection. In fact, too many countries' "democracy" has become so indirect that individuals perceive the state as an entity exercising *its* sovereignty over them.

Deresponsibilization is a vicious cycle: the less one takes part in sovereignty, the less they are informed and competent and, consequently, the less they are *able* to take part in sovereignty. The end result is a politically inept individual, so illiterate about public issues that if reinvested with their power they would likely make the wrong decisions: the perfect pretext, for the politician eager for centralization, to permanently deprive the population of any power of self-determination.

Responsibility is an essential value also for individuals who make up state organs. Public offices are not mere professions: they are missions. Public officials of any rank are custodians of democracy and Society's welfare. In exercising their office, they in fact *represent* the community and must act in its exclusive interest.

The most comforting aspect of life is that whatever condition one is in is the result of their acts or omissions. When one realizes this, they regain their power. When the members of a poorly governed people recognize their individual Responsibility, they can easily grasp two fundamental truths: no political or economic system survives without individual *consent*, and they have the power to deny their own at any time.

The average individual in society is a worker, voter, consumer, and follower. Although they may (or may prefer to) consider their position unimportant, they actually hold the structurally *necessary* functions for the sustenance of the social system. The "powerful" crave their consent; otherwise they would not be scrambling to convince them with billion-dollar budget political campaigns, commercial advertising, and media propaganda.

II

THE SOCIAL MODEL

The Society of Truth is a social model that pursues the Purpose and is informed by the fundamental principles above. Outlined below are the guidelines and some solutions that can be implemented now or in the near future. Any change from the current reality to the desired one occurs *gradually*, at a speed dictated by available means and individual contribution. As Society gets closer to achieving the Purpose, structure and operation adapt to the new circumstances in accordance with the guidelines.

As long as the conflict between bodily and spiritual components dwells in Individuals, the solutions they devise may be a compromise between the two. The best solution at any given time is the one that produces the greatest advancement toward the Purpose. Upon the attainment of the Purpose, there is no conflict: there is no Freedom in the presence of conflict.

RESEARCH

The primary tool for achieving the Purpose is Research. It is understood as the theoretical and/or practical activity of investigating the subject (the Individual) or the object (the Universe). It must aim at obtaining new Knowledge that is useful for the Purpose. "Research" in other directions is a waste of resources, but in fact very few instances fall into this category and most of them contribute, even if little or indirectly, to the attainment of useful Knowledge. The use of resources must anyway be proportional to the expected utility of the research itself.

In the Society of Truth, the end does *not* justify the means: individual freedom is not sacrificed in the name of Research. A society whose individuals have no interest in Knowledge is simply doomed to extinction and to be replaced by a society better suited to Progress.

Knowledge, once obtained, must be *preserved*. Losing Knowledge is a most serious form of inefficiency and regression. Destroying Knowledge is one of the worst crimes. The implementation of a system for collecting, classifying, and preserving *all* human knowledge is of priority.

The entire setup of Society is arranged for the promotion of its most important activity: the Search for Knowledge.

EDUCATION

Knowledge is made available to individuals through Education. Individuals *apply* Knowledge to achieve the Purpose. In order to carry out further Research, the individual is educated in previously obtained Knowledge. Knowledge is the primary source of power, and Education ensures that knowledge inequality between individuals is not too pronounced. Knowledge and, thus, Education enable the individual to think and choose freely, critically, and independently.

Below is a general model of education system that could be implemented at the time of this writing. Its function is to express the constant principles that should inform Education (logicality, undogmaticity, critical thinking, individualization, and so on), while the forms of application of such principles (types and stages of Education) are relatively arbitrary and incidental.

Education is divided into formal and free Education. The former is regulated by law. It is based upon the principles of logic and source pluralism, and it does not impose dogma. It is arranged in three stages: Basic (the same for all), Elective (subjects of choice), and Higher (university or equivalent). The first two are compulsory. Once students have learned the basics, such as reading and writing, elementary math, and a basic vocabulary, they move through the curriculum individually, at their own pace, albeit within a maximum and minimum time limit. The latter guarantees that the individual takes part in the usual social and recreational activities that are necessary for their personal development, and that competition does not replace the real purpose of Education: the transmission of Knowledge for the achievement of the Purpose. If any study time is left, it is occupied with practice: material experience is always useful to refine one's skills, even for the best professional. The individual can always enjoy free Education outside the hours of formal Education, how and when they like.

The principal education media are books, workshops, and multimedia (videos, interactive software, and the like). The use of multimedia is subject to all necessary precautions to prevent the so-called *computer vision syndrome* (dizziness, headaches, eyestrain, etc.). Secondary education media are lectures, trips, and any other useful and appropriate means. During study hours, Tutors are there and help students when they have doubts or difficulties.

Individual Education is more effective than traditional teaching for several reasons. Based on the premise that each individual is unique and different from any other, individual Education prevents the social leveling that results from forcing individuals who are better or worse endowed than the average individual to the speed and content tolerated by the latter: Education must allow each individual to realize their maximum potential.

Individuals of the same biological age may stand at very different maturity levels. Maturity is not measured in terms of experience, but rather as the degree of self- and other-awareness, whether resulting from experience or not. Every person is worthy of equal consideration and respect regardless of their age.

Oral teaching to a classroom cannot be "stopped and rewound", thus a more or less substantial portion of the information is lost during the transmission to the individual.

Traditional teaching is subject to human error when teachers themselves do not fully understand or know a concept they are to teach. The very term "teaching" suggests a passive activity on the part of the student and their subordinate position to a "more educated" individual. Education, on the contrary, must be an *active* function, whose protagonist is the student. Education professionals, as or equally to civil servants, do not just perform a job, but a socially valuable *mission*. They must be selected for proven *theoretical* knowledge and *practical* competence. The value of their contribution to society is among the highest, and their remuneration must be commensurate with it.

Formal Education, in particular Elective Education, must include at least as much practice as theory. Theory is learned through activities such as reading, listening, and observation. Practice is done through writing and speaking (in language learning), math exercise, drawing, workshops, work, use of professional tools, and so on.

At the time of this writing, it is reasonable to devote 40 hours per week to formal Education. If this limit is reached, the assignment of homework must not be allowed.

Compulsory formal Education consists of three parts: Social, Vocational, and General Education. Social Education is given to all individuals with the same content and it deals with the Fundamentals of Society (the Purpose, core values, and so on), the rights and duties of the individual within it, and the political and administrative setup. Each individual must be aware of the social system in which they participate.

In compliance with the rule of *division of functions*, Vocational Education is given according to the individual's vocation and free choice. The individual's function in Society is a basic aspect of their personal development and maturation. Vocational

Education also applies to *lycées*, i.e. schools preparing students for non-compulsory Higher Education, and it includes the basics of the professions relevant to the course of study. Admission to Higher Education is not tied to the courses one chooses for Vocational Education, but it may be subject to obtaining an intermediate preparatory degree: the individual can always "revise" their vocation.

General Education fosters individual culture and it includes the classic school subjects: languages, mathematics, history, and so on. The goal of General Education is an individual equipped with enough knowledge to observe, evaluate, and act independently in their surroundings.

GOVERNMENT AND ADMINISTRATION

DEMOCRACY

Democracy is a synonym of *popular sovereignty*, from Greek *dêmos* "the people" and *krátos* "power, sovereignty". It is currently regarded as the form of government in which sovereignty belongs to the people, who exercise it directly (direct democracy) or through freely elected representatives (indirect democracy).

It can rightly be argued that a state led by one person or a small group thereof of immense wisdom and goodness are better forms of government than *current* democracies. However, human society has yet to prove that it can infallibly identify the best leaders and these, even when they ascended to positions of power, have hardly ever been able to establish a government that would deservingly succeed them on a lasting basis.

Actually, the fact that an "enlightened" monarchy or oligarchy is more appealing than a democracy is an indication of how society is far from achieving the Purpose. In a truly advanced society, individual ability, ethics, and independent thinking are so great that there is no need to delegate decisions to one individual or group. One could say that, upon the final achievement of the Purpose, individuals' ability, rationality, and freedom would be such that the social structure itself would lose any utility and it would end. Society is a *tool* for achieving the

Purpose and, as such, it has no reason to survive the completion of its function. Democracy itself would be superseded and individuals would live in a state of *Individual Sovereignty*.

The Universe shows a cyclical nature, which even human activities do not seem to escape from. Democracy is essentially a phase in the cycle of human organization evolution. This, like all cycles, proceeds gradually, with each stage seamlessly fading into the next one. If we agreed to consider the *beginning* of the cycle as the stage of *conflictual* individual sovereignty where the law of the strongest is in force (the so-called *state of nature*), this would be followed, in this order, by centralized sovereignty (headed by "the strongest" established at the previous stage: the monarch or oligarchs), democracy (sovereignty of all individuals as a group), and *rational* individual sovereignty, where each individual's potential is fully realized, so that they no longer perceive others as threats. At this point, however, the introduction of a destabilizing external factor into the system (loss of knowledge, external attack, and the like) can bring individuals back to the beginning of the cycle.

While going through the Sovereignty Cycle's stages, Truth, Freedom, and Responsibility increase for the Individual. On closer inspection, the three principles are not only the effect of progress, they are also its cause. Active individual interest in knowledge and in the protection of freedom rights as well as the desire to take responsibility in the management of public affairs are the primary stimulus to advancement along the Cycle. In contrast, disinterest and irresponsibility are the main reasons for regression.

So, in a society that wishes to evolve towards Individual Sovereignty, the Individual must prove to be up to the responsibility entrusted to them (by democracy, for example) in order not to regress, and they must aspire to and prepare for greater responsibility in order to progress. Nurturing individual Responsibility is an essential task of the education system.

On this topic, it is worth noting that a fervent campaign against electoral abstention is taking place in several countries. The passion and unanimity of politicians and activists in general, from all sides, in support of this cause is so exceptional that their actual motivation comes through: the need for legitimacy. Indeed, in a democratic system, the individual vote legitimizes the existing political scene, no matter how bad or corrupt this is.

The individual who does not feel represented at all by any party or candidate, even with a view to voting for the least harm, is absolutely free not to go to the polls. At the same time, they have the Responsibility to act in order to produce the change they believe is necessary.

It is interesting to note how some of the most zealous anti-abstentionists, upon electoral defeat, question the entire democratic system and accuse the people of incompetence and ignorance. The solution to citizens' inability, if real, is not regression to monarchy or oligarchy (which technocracy is a version of), but *educating* the individual and reconfiguring the administrative and political system to make it more inclusive and responsibilizing.

Democracy is *formally* adopted by the vast majority of the World's countries, but it is legally configured and implemented in very different ways. Each type of democracy is located at a specific point in the Sovereignty Cycle. Direct democracies and democracies valuing minorities are closest to the Individual Sovereignty stage.

Article 1 of the Constitution of the People's Republic of China establishes a socialist state subject to the "people's democratic dictatorship". Although the use of the terms "democratic" and "dictatorship" may appear as one of the many contradictions of communism, the phrase can be interpreted as totalitarian subjection to the majority will of the people. This deprives the minority of any function in the political process. Since this is an indirect democracy, dictatorship is exercised by the governing bodies and, in fact, by the Communist Party of China.

The individual rights recognized by western Constitutions, which descend from the U.S. Constitution (in particular from the Bill of Rights containing the first ten amendments), represent monumental achievements and express touching rationality and humanity, if one considers the legal and factual condition of Man in previous millennia. The content of these Constitutions shows their authors' effort to depart from previous reality, personal impulses, and opinions, to make room for reason; it certainly does not reflect the average person's awareness and sentiment at the time of their writing. However, most of such Constitutions establish indirect democracies which, by legal configuration or manner of implementation, ended up alienating the individual from the state and limiting the actual democraticness of their systems.

The absence of legislative referenda in the Italian system is simply absurd: how can one invest the legislative power in the Parliament, whose only function is to represent the will of the people, and deny that same power to the people, the *represented*? The claim that parliamentarians are endowed with greater awareness and competence than the average person is no acceptable justification. Such alleged qualities would potentially be necessary for a law's abrogation, which can instead be decided by abrogative referendum. The elected's mandate of representation could not, in any case, allow them to depart from the will of the people in the name of an alleged intellectual superiority. Such a system is oligarchy, not democracy.

It would be equally unacceptable to justify such absurdity with the *division of functions* in the name of efficiency. Laws affect the existence of all individuals and therefore are not beyond their purview. The fact that Italy frantically employs national laws, in order to regulate special situations rather than general cases of national interest, is another aberration of its political structure which, in fact, spoils such instruments. Using national statutes to set detailed regulations overloads the legislative apparatus and warrants repeated derogations from previous statutes, thus complicating the regulatory framework beyond measure. National statutes, in national law, are second only to the Constitution and constitutional laws in the hierarchy of laws and must therefore be general and lasting in nature.

Western countries also provide examples of *de facto* aberrations in their democracies. The rigid American two-party system, based on the opposition between two broad and well-established groups, is an oversimplification of democracy that limits voters' freedom of choice. A two-party system also facilitates control by external influences which, by directly or indirectly supporting both parties, secure powerful positions regardless of the election outcome.

The wealth of economic interests around public office has produced many "professional" politicians. Some of them have little to no work experience and support themselves for all or most of their "careers" with political functions within local or national bodies or parties. Their primary activity is *selling* ideas, mostly others', which they understand or not, which they believe in or not, which they mostly do not implement, in exchange for votes. The skills they cultivate are eloquence, persuasion, and campaign strategy: the last one is often delegated to consultants. One of their few recurring qualities is ambition, though vain, when unaccompanied by competence and Purpose, and megalomaniac, when inept and craving. Thus democracy becomes pretense serving personal ends.

Politics in many countries has become a TV show, whose protagonists seem to have forgotten the most basic principles of respect and fairness. Factions uncritically oppose each other's proposals. A fan clash is staged, as if they forgot that *everybody*'s interests are at stake and that a country is one team.

Several Western democracies are in a stalemate due to weak or virtually absent majority. Accidental or planned, the result is the democracy's ineffectiveness. Decisions are not made, election promises are not realized, and sovereignty is not exercised. Thus politicians end up in the "fortunate" position where they receive salaries and allowances without having to act, take responsibility for decisions and actions, or account for broken election promises. Instead of recognizing how serious the economic and social consequences of such stagnation are and seeking compromises with the other parties, they keep on staging their pitiful show, made of quarrels and obstructionism, posing as passionate champions of party ideologies that have in fact disappeared for decades. The opposition between the right and the left wing is an outdated and artificial concept whose only effect is to divide people.

The national system that is closest to direct democracy, both legally and *de facto*, is the Swiss one. It is the first in the world as to number of referendums. It is the only one currently set up as a *directorial* republic, in which a collegial executive body (the Federal Council) consists of members of each of the major parties and serves as the Head of State. This form is not necessarily the best, but it is an excellent solution when power centralization by one individual threatens democracy and social wellbeing. Members of Parliament meet in four regular sessions per year, lasting three weeks each, and for the rest of the time (except for extraordinary sessions) they go about their respective professions. This facilitates contact with the population and awareness of the needs of the working world and society at large.

Swiss citizens are constantly called upon to express their will on local and national issues. Their interest and competence in the topics being discussed at any given time demonstrate how an *inclusive* decision-making system is also responsibilizing. The choices they make are sensible and dictated by collective interest, not by mere individual economic interest, as proved by the result of the 2018 referendum denying the TV-radio tax abolition. At the same time, citizens are free to decide on proposals that would sound like fantasy in other countries: in 2019, Zurich citizens approved tax cuts for legal entities.

The pluralism found in the Federal Council is also found at all the other levels of the system. Confrontation between parties is mostly marked by respect and dialogue, and it pursues collective agreement, knowing that the whole community will suffer if that is not achieved.

FEDERATION

In order to facilitate the exercise of popular sovereignty and make citizens socially and politically responsible, administration must be informed by the principle of *decentralization.*

In some current legal systems, including Italy's (Const. Art. 117), local authorities' powers are conceived as residual in relation to the national state's. In such a "centralist" model, powers are allocated with a preference for the highest (national) level, going gradually down to peripheral entities, which are entrusted with lesser tasks.

In a decentralized system, the approach is reversed: powers are assigned first and mainly to local authorities. Powers of a general or coordinating nature (such as Defense) are entrusted to higher bodies. Such systems can be found in some federal republics. Switzerland, in particular, is again a good example: according to the principle of *subsidiarity* characterizing its constitutional system, functions are assigned to a higher level (Canton, Federal Government) only if it is capable of performing them significantly better than subordinate levels (Municipality, Canton).

Decentralization enables individuals to participate directly and actively in the management of their surroundings. Their expressions of will find quick implementation in front of their eyes. Thus, their interest in and sense of belonging to the community are strengthened.

Every region has its own needs and potential, which are respectively best addressed and made use of by those who know them best: the local governments. A system that collects the will of millions of individuals belonging to local contexts as diverse as those of Italy and attempts to devise solutions applicable to the entire national territory by making a rough average of such contexts — which it does not even know — is, to say the least, much less efficient than a decentralized system, if not a total failure.

Federation is the arrangement that currently best suits the principle of decentralization and is situated at a later stage in the Sovereignty Cycle than centralized democracies, as it is closer to Individual Sovereignty. Decentralization is not to be confused with feudalism: the hierarchy of laws remains unchanged and governed by the fundamental principles of the Constitution, i.e. the rights of individuals.

The assumption that a federal system undermines a nation's unity is refuted by facts. Separatist sentiments prove more vigorous in unitary states, such as the United Kingdom, Italy, and Spain (this is the case in Scotland, Lombardy-Veneto, Sardinia, Catalonia, the Basque Country, and so on), than in federal states such as the United States, Germany, and Switzerland itself, because here local communities' interests enjoy greater consideration. Such sentiments do not stem from discriminatory tendencies, but rather from the country's *fiscal*, economic, and/or political setup.

Racism has been used throughout history as an "ideological" justification for movements that were born for economic reasons. The number of individuals who sincerely deny others' rights in the name of biological superiority is extremely small.

Cultural differences do not seem to be the cause of separatisms either: within the borders of some federal states (such as Canada and, again, Switzerland) even different languages are spoken.

Separatism (or secessionism) is understood as a movement inspired by the desire to separate from a nation to which one belongs by shared language, culture, traditions, and the like, and it should not be confused with the independentism of nations that were conquered, subjugated, or unified by invading forces.

Separatism has obvious disadvantages. First of all, it is mostly accompanied by antagonism or at least indifference towards others, which limit individual and collective potential. Unless forcibly belonging to a depraved nation, every local community as well as every individual should base their conduct on the principle of *solidarity*, which is understood as the feeling of belonging to one same entity. Within every group there are differences. If these were to be consistently resolved by separation, individuals would eventually end up alone.

The fracturing of a nation can result in major economic repercussions, which must be considered alongside the expected effects of separation. It reduces economies of scale. Unless trade — which has just transformed from national to international — is quickly reorganized, it would suffer a decline, resulting in a loss of wealth (meant as available amount of economic utility).

It is a fact that, currently, the major global powers are also the largest and/or most populous countries: there is no doubt that the World's equilibrium is in the hands of the United States, Russia, and China. *Quantity* is an essential factor in the order of powers and influences. Separation limits a nation's weight in the international arena and thus its ability to influence humankind's direction. Such weight originates primarily from the total economic and defensive available resources. Separation is an extreme measure, which federation should be preferred to whenever possible.

The border between separatism and independence is a blurred line. Today's geopolitical situation is largely the result of actions considered by contemporary thinking as injustices committed against pre-existing nations. If one were to engage in reconstructing such events, going back to the dawn of human civilization, they would end up questioning the entire atlas.

Present situations are to be addressed in the present and considering present and future effects of the devised solutions, while complying with the principle of self-determination. Peoples once united coercively which, today, together, reasonably meet the definition of *nation*, regardless of historical causes, should prefer federation to what would otherwise be the pursuit of separation rather than independence.

In a fair federal system, tax revenues are determined, collected, and used for the most part at the local level. This stimulates production, positive work culture, and innovation, as it allows individuals to directly see and enjoy the fruits of their efforts. A virtuous circle is generated that increases the system's wealth, thus also allowing the financing of social security for those who really need to resort to it. The only way to help less productive communities is to stimulate their work culture and support them in adopting healthy and efficient economic systems.

Inefficient systems naturally transform or end. Heavy redistribution of tax revenues in favor of less productive regions is doubly ineffective: on the one hand it artificially perpetuates a system otherwise set to change spontaneously, on the other it frustrates enterprises and workforce in the more industrious areas, thus reducing their productivity. A hard-working individual who is not allowed to enjoy utility in proportion to their production will not stay so for long: this is the ruin of communism.

The wealth gap between northern and southern Italy, after more than 150 years of national unity, is an example of how economic homogeneity is anything but typical of unitary states.

Federation is an application of the principle of division of functions in politics and administration. Local governments have access to a much greater amount of detailed information than central bodies have, and they *specialize* in the matters they deal with within the territory they are responsible for.

A federal system allows local communities to effectively manage and exploit the potential of their own contexts, while also countering social leveling, that is, the simplification and standardization of a nation's culture, economy, knowledge, traditions, thinking, skills, and customs. *Diversity* is a well-known asset in biology and it is a source of survival and progress.

The advantages of a federal system do not justify supernational initiatives to impose the joining of different nations into a single federation. The right of self-determination of peoples is inviolable. Any decision to merge separate countries should be adopted by referendum with a *quorum* and qualified majority.

THE ECONOMY

PRINCIPLES

The economy is the framework of every society. Regardless of its form, its function does not change. It provides for Society and its members and it fuels Research. It is understood as the totality of group or individual *production activities* and of *exchanges* between its members (organizations and individuals).

The result of production as well as the object of exchange is *utility*: whenever new utility is generated for Society or for the individual, an economically relevant act is being performed. Exchange also meets this definition, because the parties' intention to exchange goods or services is based on the prospect of increasing individual utility: if one trades a chair for a lamp, it means that the lamp is more *useful* to him or her than the chair; the same, conversely, is true for the other party, who prefers the chair to the lamp.

Tangible or intangible objects having utility are called *goods*. All individuals are involved in the economy most of their time, as utility producers, exchangers, and consumers. *Wealth* and *poverty* are understood as abundance or lack of available utility.

The economy should be informed by the basic principles of Truth, Freedom, and Responsibility.

Every economy is based on trust between actors. The rate of trade, and thus that of the creation of new utility, is proportional to the amount of trust. Without trust, there is no exchange. An economy based on truth allows the highest degree of trust in the system: the parties in each exchange have perfect knowledge of the utility of the goods being exchanged and therefore can make the most efficient choices.

Economic freedom allows first and foremost each individual to pursue their professional vocation. Freedom of exchange allows goods to circulate in the market and be used at their highest utility, thus ensuring the best *resource allocation*. Each good will be traded as long as there is an actor ascribing greater utility to it than the previous purchaser did, and it will eventually be *consumed* (used) by the one who can get the maximum utility from it.

Tax measures on trade can alter goods' relative utility — think of excise on certain products — and should therefore be carefully vetted to avoid affecting resource allocation *efficiency*. Efficiency is the ratio of resources you use to the utility you obtain. Maximum efficiency is achieved when maximum utility is obtained with the least use of resources.

Public services, that is, the minimum essential services for an active individual and social existence at any given stage of progress of Society, should be provided by public organizations on a non-exclusive basis. They should include, at the time of this writing, communication (mail and telephone/internet), information (newspapers, radio, television), movement (transportation), as well as individual health, banking, and insurance services. By virtue of economic freedom, any company is free to operate in the market of such services. Public organizations cannot make a *profit* and cannot be subsidized with tax revenues. They offer services at cost price — which includes research and innovation costs and security reserves — thereby securing a competitive advantage on price over private actors equal to the profit they would make if they were private. The presence of private companies and the prohibition of financial support from the government put constant pressure on public organizations, forcing them to pursue efficiency.

Health care and insurance services present peculiar issues. Profits in both sectors depend partially or entirely on the occurrence of undesirable events. Health care businesses (hospitals, pharmaceutical companies, and so on) earn profit from individuals' illness and injuries. The demand for their services is a negative event in itself. In order to avoid a conflict between private interests in high demand and profit and the collective interest in individuals' welfare, health care services must therefore be provided also and primarily by public organizations. Prices for such services should be equal to their cost and not proportional to the severity of the illness or injury.

Likewise, insurance companies profit from the fear of an adverse event taking place. The demand for their services is directly proportional to the threat level perceived in one's environment. This could make the collective interest in safety clash with the private interest in a dangerous environment (or perceived as such by the public). In such a scenario, an insurance company could at the very least exclude programs against juvenile delinquency from its charity sponsoring initiatives, for example. If it is affiliated with information companies (newspapers, TV networks, and the like), e.g. through common shareholders, news may be communicated in a more alarming tone than it should. Of course, even very serious misconduct can result from such a conflict of interest: the more serious the more significant the economic interests at stake and the resulting pressures. At least essential individual insurance services and those mandatory for all must be provided also and primarily by public organizations.

By virtue of freedom of (economic and non-economic) private initiative, public services can be provided not only by public organizations and private companies but also by *private public-service organizations*. These, like public organizations, are companies necessarily bound by the break-even requirement — i.e. revenues must balance out costs — and cannot produce profits. Salaries and active sponsorships are limited by law to prevent the perversion of their primary purpose. They are also an expression of the individual freedom to help: help can be conceived as a *contribution without profit*. They cannot receive private or public financial support.

Free enterprise is a fundamental right of every individual. It is the freedom to independently undertake temporary or permanent economic ventures, using one's own means or paid ones (labour and capital) and receiving the fruits directly. It guarantees the possibility of realizing one's production potential and enjoying the results of one's efforts and merits. Any system protecting this right triggers a virtuous circle in which each individual, motivated by the proportionality between their work and the gains coming from it, seeks to produce further utility.

Enterprise is the fundamental instrument of resource allocation and organization, and thus of utility production. The utility increase in an economic system as a result of establishing an enterprise is exponential, since it enables other individuals to establish enterprises in turn, which produce and exchange utility with the first one, or to produce utility and be paid for it as employees.

Law and administration must protect and promote free enterprise and its exercise, *de jure* and *de facto*, by *sustainable taxation*, adequate training programs, a sound and efficient capital supply system, safeguarding of competition, and clear and lean administrative requirements and duties. The reality in some countries is the opposite: the state overburdens businesses with excessive taxes; a heavy bureaucracy, unaware of its function, slows down and discourages private initiative; a minimal part of education is devoted to the *creation* of entrepreneurs. Small- and medium-sized firms, tied to the local economy and unable (unlike large multinational companies) to divert profits to more favorable foreign tax systems, die at the expense of competition and *diversity*, which is an essential value in economics too.

The value of enterprise is so obvious that it is hard to conceive that a politician could adopt policies that do not favor it or even penalize it, all the more so when they are established economists, so much so that malice seems a more likely reason than incompetence.

As Society approaches a state of Individual Sovereignty, individual financial freedom grows and enterprise becomes the dominant production model, replacing employment. Individuals start owning their *production input* and exchange this freely. In fact, financial freedom can be understood, in practical terms, as having enough financial resources to be able to freely determine the allocation of one's work. Financial freedom is a very important measure of Progress.

A system that promotes individual indebtedness for the satisfaction of induced consumerist "needs", overburdens taxpayers, neglects vocational education, or otherwise diminishes individual financial potential, is in fact *limiting* financial freedom, that is, it is forcing the individual to allocate their production input to activities they would avoid, on terms they would not accept. The individual finds themselves trapped in a job that does not fulfill them and may end up hating work and production. Since these occupy most of their usable time, they may fall into a state of deep frustration. The consequences are dire: unable to change their environment, the individual tries to change their perception of it by using drugs, psychiatric drugs, and alcohol. The final outcome is an addicted individual, whose personality and awareness are clouded.

UTILITY, PRODUCTION AND MONEY

Money is the tool for facilitating the exchange of utility between individuals. It is assigned an agreed value, recognized by a group of individuals, which makes it accepted as a medium of exchange. Thus its only utility is exchangeability and it is subject to fluctuations depending on exchange rates, inflation, and so on.

The agreed utility of money does not replace the *real* utility which it is exchanged for. When new money is issued by central banks, loaves of bread, cars, or buildings do not instantly appear. Money is exchanged for *existing* commodities, which in turn are transformed into finished goods. In the absence of real utility to exchange money for, this gets completely useless. When the ratio of real utility to money (*purchasing power*) decreases, as when new money is put into the system without equivalent new real utility being produced, money itself (including money already in the system) loses value, thus making those who have it poorer: inflation.

One of the problems with the current economic system is indeed the remuneration of an individual or group for production that does not take place. Welfarism, promoted by parties with no better arguments to win people's votes, rewards unproductiveness, thus bringing a country, in few years, into such a lack of resources (utility) that these are not even enough for those who actually need and are entitled to receive them. Indeed, the ratio of utility to money diminishes: if welfare money is newly issued, there is an increase in the amount of money; if welfare money is taken away from businesses and workers with higher taxes, production is discouraged and utility decreases. At the same time, on a subjective level, employment is disincentivized by rewarding unproductive individuals, so that the population on average becomes less productive and, again, available utility diminishes.

Similarly, it happens that a listed firm is paid before it has actually realized the equivalent output, based on the expectation that it will do so in the future. As a result of aggressive advertising and propaganda campaigns, shares are traded at a total price of 40 times a company's net worth and 750 times its yearly profit. Thus the entrepreneur's financial wealth increases dozens of times before they have actually produced an equivalent amount of utility. Like the individual maintained by the welfare state although being able to work, the entrepreneur who is rewarded too early has no incentive to produce. It does not necessarily mean that the entrepreneur will ruin the company, but at least their effort and caution may be reduced. The greater the early compensation, the bigger the risk that expected production will not materialize.

The current public capital market's structure, where the profit of those who invest in company shares (stock) derives primarily from *capital gain* (increase in value over the purchase price) rather than from the company's income (paid to investors in the form of *dividends*), shows the laziness and greed of a financial system whose attention has been diverted from production and has gotten stuck on money. The market value of stocks is set by *expectations*, a company's income is the result of its *production*. Production is the *cause*, utility and the equivalent money are the *effect*. The belief that one can get rich without production, in a lasting and sustainable way, is naive or criminal. Taxation that hits income more than capital gains can be qualified by the same adjectives.

In order for the financial system to be efficient and sustainable, its actors have the Responsibility to adopt a conduct that is conscious of its systemic effects and not to seek mere short-term individual profit. They must be *competent* and know the nature of the relationship between production and money. Given the influence of information on stock exchanges, they must be able to identify conflicts of interest in its sources. For example, if Newspaper X, controlled by Investor Y, published news that affected the market value of Listed Company Z, in turn controlled by Investor Y, how reliable would such news be? As to rating agencies and auditing companies, they are remunerated for their services by the same companies they rate and audit.

Since this is a (capital) *market*, the laws of supply and demand apply. The merchandise being traded is expectations, not finished products, and those are deeply affected by *opinions* besides facts. When one buys a share in a company located thousands of miles away, knowing only financial data and ratings whose certification is subject to conflict of interest, the transaction risk is very high. So we say one is "playing the stock market", but how reasonable is it to make the financing of *pro-*

duction, society's means of survival and growth, dependent on gambling?

As discussed, the expectation traded by the investor is not so much the business success of the company as its share price increase. Although related, the two events do not necessarily correspond. The former is determined by the production and sale of utility, with profit. The price increase of a company's stock is the result of both the first event and market dynamics. Supply and demand are strongly influenced by opinions, news, rumors, and trends fueled by the media, analysts, and investors themselves. This is how entrepreneurial risk, which is typical of any business, has been exacerbated and turned into *gambling*.

The current financial system is anyway the result of the interest of few people making astronomical profits from it. One market control lever they use, again, is opinion. Let's assume that the large Investment Bank A buys a large amount of Company B's stock. The other large banks — assuming that there is perfect competition among them, although this is unlikely given the mutual cross-shareholdings — intrigued by the transaction, decide to follow the first bank, although with smaller purchases, so as not to deny themselves the opportunity for potential profit. Bank A owns shares in several newspapers, which soon publish the news about the purchases. Small investors, relying on the expertise of each big bank's large team of analysts, follow in turn. Bank A has been working with Rating Agency X and Auditing Firm Y for years and, thanks to the influence it now has over Company B, makes this buy services from them too. Agency X and Firm Y are aware of the possibility that, by denying high scores and account certifications to B, they would jeopardize the relationship with an important client such as A. So it is obvious how, regardless of the company's productivity and solvency, such a mechanism generates positive expectations among investors and thus an increase in demand and stock price.

Opinion can also be used to produce or amplify price fluctuations in order to generate further profits by buying and selling the same stock repeatedly.

Once traders recognize an effective source of profit, they try to raise as much capital as possible to allocate to it. For this purpose, they may issue bonds or use other financial instruments. One technique that banks have historically resorted to is securitization, which is the transformation of their own receivables into marketable securities. A typical example is the issuance of bonds backed by receivables from real estate mortgages. In this way, banks get immediate liquidity based on receivables due in the future. This mechanism can incentivize banks to lend money in order to increase their receivables and turn them into liquidity right away. When a bank, or rather the individuals who run it (and are interested in their own immediate profits rather than in the survival of the institution they work for and the health of the economic system), care more about immediate liquidity than about the soundness of the underlying credit, large losses loom for savers.

Strictly speaking, with the exception of money paid to a company to purchase newly issued securities and used for production, money invested in the purchase of stock does not constitute *capital* to the extent that the company's price deviates from the value of its actual production capacity. Capital, in the proper sense, is all the means employed in production, in the form of money, machinery, and so on. When you buy a share in a company at a price above its value, you pay the capital back to the initial investor, plus a capital gain equal to the increase in the company's production capacity, *plus* a capital gain not corresponding to any production capacity increase. This goes beyond the very concept of *finance*, which is understood as any activity of raising capital to be used in production.

Profit generated by capital is the result of production. Profit from capital gain that is not proportional to a company's production capacity is just speculation, and it will correspond to another investor's loss as soon as the disproportion becomes known and the company's price falls.

Because of goods' consumption and decay, the production of new utility is necessary in order to at least maintain the total available amount of utility in the system. When expected production does not occur, the entire system gets poorer, that is, overall it loses a certain amount of available utility.

EXCHANGE

As discussed above, *exchange* plays a fundamental role, and the value of money as a tool lies exactly in facilitating it. In order to achieve the Purpose, which entails the maximum realization of individual potential and freedom, exchange must be *fair*, that is, the utility being exchanged must be approximately equivalent within a common reference system (objective utility or market value) and it must carry the features promised during the negotiation to provide the expected subjective utility. The latter is necessarily different for each party, otherwise exchange would not take place.

Some say that "business is done by two", meaning that both parties must benefit from an exchange. This promotes the best allocation of resources. On the contrary, a system marked by unfair exchange limits individuals' financial freedom by constantly taking utility away from them. The ultimate version of such a system trend is slavery.

Money *does not* disappear from the economy. In the current monetary system, in simplified terms, money is issued by the central bank in the form of loans to commercial banks, against interest x. Commercial banks in turn lend the money to businesses and people at an interest $x + y$. Profit made by the central bank (x) goes mainly to the government and to a lesser extent to commercial banks, which own a share in the central bank. When the population perceives a decrease in its purchasing power (i.e. its possession of exchangeable utility), it normally means that the exchange system has been intentionally or accidentally upset. Non-production is the first example of unfair exchange.

Another phenomenon upsetting exchange is *consumerism*, i.e. the tendency to consume more utility than necessary, so that the utility derived from consumption is far less than the value of the good being consumed, that is, the marginal utility of new consumption is minimal. Marginal utility is the utility of an additional unit of the same good, for example the utility of a second car. Clearly, the utility of a car for an individual without one would be greater than the utility the same individual would derive from owning a second identical one.

For example, an individual owns a two-year-old sofa. They are targeted by a furniture company's advertising campaign suggesting that a new sofa in the living room (of the same production quality and price as the one they own, but with a new design) "will be loved by guests". Thus they decide to buy it.

While the marginal utility of the new sofa is minimal, the individual has deprived themselves of financial means (hence purchasing power, hence utility) equal to the objective utility of the good, which is approximately equivalent to the utility that an individual who owns no sofa would have gotten from it. Basically, the individual has purchased "a piece" of a sofa's utility, for the price of a whole sofa. Since the used sofa, being a consumer good, has suffered a decline in market value for resale that is larger than the new sofa's marginal utility (or will simply end up in the attic), the net result is a loss of utility for the individual: they get poorer. Add to the scenario that the furniture company offers a financing service, so that the individual lacking enough purchasing power in the present commits to additional costs (interest), that is, further loss of available utility: the decrease of individual wealth in the current consumerist market is evident.

Non-production and consumerism, causing an overall loss of utility in the system, generate inflation, which can in turn be the cause of a further exchange inequity: underpayment. A worker who agrees to a certain wage at a given moment will see the purchasing power of their wage (unless this is constantly adjusted) and money *savings* decline by the inflation rate.

These and every other kind of exchange imbalance cause social regression in the direction of financial slavery: making an individual poorer limits their freedom of choice in the allocation of their production, forcing them to work in activities and under conditions they would otherwise refuse, to the advantage of a small group of individuals. These, when lacking any social spirit, actively seek to promote and consolidate an unfair exchange system in order to secure and increase such advantage.

Parliaments and governments must make laws and implement economic policies supporting a financial system based on the production of real utility, rather than on money. Solutions deriving from this approach are countless.

Income and dividends from production should be subject to the lowest possible taxation and in any case lower than that on capital gains, so as to encourage business managers to remunerate investors in a stable, lasting, and sustainable way with profits generated by production, rather than by stock appreciation.

Proportion between tax revenue and utility provided to the population must always be maintained. Overtaxation is a clear example of unfair exchange and, as such, again makes people poorer and limits their freedom.

Issuance of new money should be to enterprises and reserved for production, for example by tying it to certain budget items (purchase of machinery, hiring labor, etc.) for a specific period of time. Enterprises in turn will pay workers, who can buy the newly produced utility, thus remunerating enterprises and fueling further production: the virtuous circle of production.

Wealth redistribution through high taxation is a chimera, as it discourages production and consequently makes society poorer, besides causing capital flight to more favorable foreign taxation.

A country where the government deprives the individual of half of the fruits of their production is a country where people have lost sovereignty long ago. Sadly, many Western countries fit more or less exactly this description, including the United States, historically a guardian of economic freedom and individual freedom in general.

The Robinhoodian paradigm of wealth redistribution must be replaced by that of *general enrichment*: by virtue of what right can one deprive the "rich" of the fruits of their production? Everybody's wealth should rather be increased, by increasing available utility in the system by production. Nothing makes it impossible that, one day, everyone will be able to drive a sports car.

On closer inspection, the "rich" affected by overtaxation are mostly owners of small- and medium-sized businesses and professional firms (millionaires at most), whose production is tied to their home region; on the contrary, billionaires reside in low-tax countries or exploit *ad hoc* tax expedients to escape normal taxation. This is the case with private foundations in the United States and foreign trusts for British citizens, as well as with the flat income tax for new residents in Italy: those who move there can opt for a fixed tax of 100,000 euros per year, a minimal sum for multimillion-dollar incomes, which humbles some of the best-known "tax havens". The goal this initiative is formally based on is to attract foreign capital. The truth is that those who benefit from it are not obliged to relocate their business, nor do they have any incentive to do so, given the terrible conditions Italian companies are subject to. The only capital the new resident is required to import is equal to their personal consumption plus the tax itself, which is ridiculously low compared to the rates applied to the rest of the taxpayers: a shameless insult by the state to its citizens.

Some billionaires and their crony entourages exert their influence in order to grow and consolidate their privileges, generating a vicious circle of inequity. They sneakily control the media and support typically leftist causes, in order to gain people's approval and weaken the upper middle class, which represents individual financial freedom and thus the primary threat to their power. There is nothing wrong with being a billionaire; on the contrary, in a system based on merit and justice, wealth is an indicator of productivity and ability. The social value of a successful enterprise is discussed exhaustively above. However, there is no justification for those who promote a deceptive and oppressive system to maintain or increase wealth and power, at the expense of other individuals.

$$\dot{=}$$

SPIRITUALITY

The human individual's composition of spirit and body has always been reflected in the idea that two distinct worlds exist: the spiritual and the physical one. Both worlds are subject to sovereignty: spiritual and secular. The two sovereignties can be held by one or two different entities. The first case is that of the Pope, who holds both spiritual power over the Christian community and temporal power over the Vatican State, and some Middle Eastern governments. The second one is that of secular states.

Spiritual sovereignty actually belongs to an entity (or entities) that individuals identify as the Creator, whom religious authorities are representatives of.

Spiritual sovereignty is more cogent than physical sovereignty. It deals with thought, purposes, values, conscience. It deals with the inner nature of the individual rather than their external manifestations, which may or may not be sincere. In order to grasp this concept, it is enough to ask yourself what would worry you the most: someone controlling your thoughts or someone controlling your body?

Spiritual sovereignty is not unrelated to the Sovereignty Cycle. We can assume that the Cycle starts at a virtually animal stage where individuals have no concept of spirit. This would be followed by some awareness of their own identity and by the spiritual subjection of all individuals to one or few entities: spiritual monarchy and oligarchy, that is, monotheism and polytheism. At the beginning of this second phase, individuals mostly conceive of the spirit as something they *have*, not that they *are*, which was given to them by a god: "When I die, *my soul* will go to heaven". They regard themselves as beings of little value, completely subject to the will of a superior being distinct from them.

With Progress, individuals gain awareness of their being. The Age of Enlightenment is an example. Human reason became the movement's core theme, but the existence of a Supreme Being was not necessarily denied. Classical thinking is another example: on the one hand it marked one of the most productive times for philosophy, and on the other it believed in the existence of demigods and in a closer relationship between humans and divinity. In this respect, although it brought some progress in human rights, Christian monotheism (at least in its historical version) caused a regression in the Spiritual Sovereignty Cycle, and the Middle Ages showed the effects of that.

Going up through the various stages of the Cycle, individual spiritual awareness and freedom expand. Individuals increase confidence in their convictions and are free to believe in whatever they consider to be true, to the point where each would have their own exclusive "religion". This would be Individual Spiritual Sovereignty and is pursued through Subject Research. The individual at this point would have full self-awareness, that is, the correct answers to the typical existential questions: "Who am I?", "Where do I come from?", and so on.

The idea of a Supreme Being distinct from the self would be overcome. Each individual would be a god, meant as a ruler of the spirit.

Individuals may be one Supreme Being "divided" into independent selves belonging to the same original substance. This would correspond to the philosophical belief that Being (or God) is *infinite* and therefore is everything and everyone.

Or, each individual may be a distinct and infinite Supreme Being: the spiritual Universe may follow different laws from physical ones and allow several infinities to coexist. One could even conceive that, once Individual Spiritual Sovereignty is achieved, there would be a spiritual universe for each individual, within which they can be infinite.

Religions, as organized movements, have taken on the function of bringing individuals with similar spiritual beliefs together, increasing their knowledge of the spiritual world (according to each religion's creed), and spreading their vision. This last characteristic, known as *proselytizing*, over time has caused some mistrust and sometimes dislike towards some denominations or religion in general, even more so than political propaganda. In fact, it is totally reasonable for a group of individuals who are convinced of the goodness of their knowledge to try to share it with others, as long as this activity is carried out in the form of offering and not of imposing or abusing.

Religions contribute to Research. Virtually all major religions offer theories about the Subject and the Object. Some religious experiences produce stronger certainty in those living them than that derived from science. In fact, science produces truths within artificial models designed by Man to represent *parts* of Nature. These are total truths with reference to the model they belong to, but partial truths with respect to the *totality* of the Universe. Minor variations in models produce different truths, as demonstrated by the evolution from classical physics to quantum physics and relativistic physics.

The fact that a spiritual certainty could not be fully shared with others or demonstrated in the physical Universe would not make it less true for the individual, but neither could it be dogmatically imposed on everyone. No one should be forced to believe in something they personally do not perceive or logically understand. The blame suffered by traditional religions is also the result of the violation of this principle.

Religious and scientific research have a characteristic in common: intuition. Intuition, understood as awareness not resulting from logical evidence, is a sort of knowledge *creation*. We can assume there are different degrees of intuition, from totally spontaneous knowledge to observing correlations, analogical thinking, and so on.

Scientific research by nature tends to use intuition to take short but safe steps and thus develop theories that can be proven in a relatively near future. Indeed, the purpose of *scientific* research is the production of *science*, that is, proven knowledge.

As in any other profession, a scientist would risk their post if they did not perform their task. "Scientists" who venture into developing theories that cannot be proven in a relatively short time are, strictly speaking, *philosophers*. Philosophy is indeed the family that science, religion, and every other form of knowledge belong to. A scientist is always a philosopher, but a philosopher is not necessarily a scientist.

On the contrary, religious and philosophical research can fly to stratospheric heights on the wings of intuition and grasp magnificent truths, or crash disastrously. On the one hand, this must prevent intuitive knowledge from being forcibly implanted into individuals in the name of "faith", on the other it must deter from discrediting any knowledge that is not proven, or that cannot be proven in the immediate future, in the name of "science". Many ancient philosophical and religious concepts have found evidence in modern physics.

If not supported by far-sighted philosophical intuitions, scientific research is an unguided tool risking being applied to trivial matters. The human species does not have infinite time to evolve. Earth, the Sun, and every resource it depends on are constantly moving along their natural cycles. Some phases of these cycles will not allow Man's survival at its present stage of progress.

Religion by nature is an extremely personal subject, it deals with the individual's innermost aspects. Spiritual sovereignty is more cogent than political sovereignty: when it is exercised by criminal religious authorities, consequences are catastrophic. When extraordinary individuals' prophetic words become the levers of control of insane individuals, it is the beginning of a dark age. The fact that this has actually happened several times throughout history has betrayed individuals' trust and, together with dogmatism and the obsolescence of certain teachings and practices, it has caused new generations to move away from religions and, consequently, from spirituality.

The very word "religion" arouses some sort of repulsion in many, evoking a sense of conformism and standardization of spirituality and oppression, in utter contradiction with the goal it should naturally be associated with of increasing individual spiritual awareness through deeply personal experiences.

Einstein wrote that "science without religion is lame", as "science" started to replace religion in the Subject Research. Although impartiality and objectivity are attributed to it, even science is subject to arbitrariness, propaganda, and opinion. Clearly, these things have nothing to do with real science, but, like religion, science too is exploited to pursue ulterior motives. The result is scientists' *opinions* (a contradiction in terms) taking the part of certain political actions, contradictory "scientific" research results (a paradox), and so on.

There are entire subjects advertised as science, which are not. Medicine, for example, is defined in dictionaries as science, although it is a *practice*. Science, by definition, is *sure knowledge* within the framework of a precisely *defined* model, which allows one to predict exactly the course of an event. Medicine is an *application* of certain findings of chemical and physical science to an extremely complex and still undefined subject: the human individual. The consequence is that different individuals respond differently to the same treatments and drugs, that every decade old medical theories are disowned and new ones are worshipped. The same is true of psychology, even more so as it deals with individual mental and spiritual experiences.

The "sciences" that have replaced religion in the research on the ego are psychology and psychiatry. By etymology, the former is the "*study* of the soul", the latter is the "*healing* of the soul" and as such a branch of medicine. Both are not sciences and both underwent a materialistic drift in the second half of the last century.

Wundt, generally considered the father of modern psychology and the first academic to carry out experiments on the mind, concluded that mental and physiological (i.e. brain) processes are parallel and independent.

According to Jung:

> [T]here are these peculiar faculties of the psyche—that it isn't entirely confined to space and time. You can have dreams or visions of the future. You can see around corners and such things. Only ignorants deny these facts. It's quite evident that they

do exist and have existed always.

In contrast, mental "sciences" have increasingly focused on physiological rather than psychic treatment. Prescription of psychiatric drugs has increased at a dizzying rate since the mid-twentieth century and continues to this day. Research some time ago found that, in one year, one in six adult Americans (and one in five women) purchased a prescription psychiatric drug. It is estimated that every year 100,000 patients in the United States are treated with electroconvulsive therapy (electroshock).

It is easily observed that emotion, except in case of use of psychotropic substances, is not caused by physiological processes: the individual has an experience, which causes an emotion, which a certain physical and chemical reaction in the body corresponds to. Without the initial experience and the individual's awareness of that experience, no physiological process would take place. Treating depression, which is an emotion, with chemistry, that is, with drugs, is to try to relieve symptoms, not to *heal* the cause. This is evidenced by the fact that patients rarely stop taking antidepressants if their unhappiness has not been resolved by other methods. One might ask, then, why Research on psychic rather than physiological processes is not more vigorously promoted. The huge profits from physiological therapies might be an answer. The global turnover generated annually by psychiatric drugs and electroshocks is in the tens of billions of dollars.

The materialistic drift produces some remarkable social and economic phenomena. One's concept of themselves and of the world informs one's values and goals. According to a survey, whose result is rather predictable, atheists tend to find more existential meaning in money, hobbies, and tourism, and less in family, compared to Christians. Such tendencies evidently affect the subjects' behavior. In their decision-making process, the relative weight of money compared to other values will be greater. For example, even to a small extent, they will give more importance to profitability in choosing a profession, or wealth in choosing a partner, than other individuals. They will care a bit less about the welfare of their children. They will be willing to spend more on hobbies and travel: two markets that have grown exponentially in the last decades. In the worst case, the result may be an individual with a failing marriage, seeking relief from a job that does not fulfill them (but which they chose for pay level) in hobbies and holidays: a rather familiar pattern, isn't it?

Atheism, by definition, is not believing in the existence of God or gods and it does not necessarily entail denying the existence of individual spirits. However, in fact, atheism and materialism mostly coincide as shown by the same survey, which found that only 4% of atheists find existential meaning in spirituality.

Thus, materialism changes the individual and social relative values of life components (family, money, spirit, body, work, leisure, duty, life, death, and so on). To the change in values evidently corresponds a change in decisions. We can say that until the 1960s Western population was still strongly religious. 1968 movements triggered a trend change. Although distrust in religious institutions was justifiable and spirituality does not coincide with adherence to organized religion, disavowing traditional values was not necessarily beneficial.

Reality is much more complex than the naive or propagandists claim. Good and bad are ideas that mostly materialize in the physical world in terms of *better* and *worse*. The variables are countless. The options available to human decision are rarely completely right or wrong, they are normally better or worse than each other, and often their respective values are so similar as to make the choice hard. A bad ruler (in absolute terms) may be better than the alternatives at a given time in history. Thus, wholly rejecting a person, movement, or doctrine, because they are partly imperfect, is naive, just as it would be foolish to un-critically welcome everything that is proposed by someone who has offered something positive before.

Similarly, disavowing certain existential values because a hu-man organization with a bad reputation has promoted them (or rather, exploited them!) is quite crazy. A society's values nor-mally arise as effective solutions to real problems, they rarely are an arbitrary imposition.

Every value is to be judged objectively, independently, and in its own context of application (the present and the future). All social systems in history, including the worst dictatorships, have promoted positive (*better*) and negative (*worse*) values. The overall value of such systems is measured by the predominance of one or the other type of values *in their historical context*. Each single value should be critically examined in order to pre-serve it or abandon it.

Propaganda is ludicrous when it totally disavows past extra-ordinary personalities and doctrines in the light of modern values (or pretexts), as it denies those advancements without which the same modern values they invoke would not even ex-ist.

The change in the balance of values caused by materialism, i.e. the increased value of material goods and welfare compared to other values, produces peculiar economic behaviors. First, it causes an increase in consumption: the subjective utility of con-sumer goods for a materialist individual is higher than it is for a non-materialist individual. Second, a materialist individual on average will have a stronger tendency to seek remuneration *before* production, due to the higher value that money holds in his or her scale of values, and to make unfair exchanges, compared to a non-materialist individual.

Such behaviors bring about individual and systemic loss of utility and *loss of wealth*. As for the clergyman celebrating poverty in the name of spirituality while wallowing in luxury, the actual interests of those who promote materialism should be investigated.

The value most severely affected by materialism is that of life versus death. While promises of eternal bliss persuade people to fight and die for the ulterior motives of warmongering criminals, fear of materialistic death, that is, fear of the end of self-awareness, turns the population into a cowardly herd that is so afraid of fighting for their freedom as to see it slip through their fingers.

Fear that death represents the complete end of the ego deeply influences the individual's thinking and conduct. It causes the feeling that existence is meaningless and that it is not worth engaging in any long-term effort, because one will not enjoy the fruits of it. The individual's scope of action shrinks to the activities he or she will benefit from within the span of their lifetime *at most*. Although there may be individuals who are so altruistic as to use their energies and time for the benefit of future generations despite believing they will live only once, it is certain that the population *on average* will tend to be less far-sighted. The aforementioned survey proves it, having found that an increase in the perceived value of money, hobbies, and tourism among atheists is accompanied by a decrease in the value of family, which is the most direct expression of interest in future generations.

The fear of materialistic death can result in the *terror* of losing the only existence one can have. The individual becomes on average more tame and compliant. They do not react unless it is absolutely necessary. They hold on to their job to secure their livelihood, at the cost of compromising with other values. They become hypochondriacal and anxious. They are less inclined to intervene to stop an instance of pickpocketing or other injustice. Heroism is replaced by opportunism.

The decay and death of the body are part of life, either because of the organism's inability to do otherwise or necessity for the survival of the species. The second hypothesis would be supported by the fact that genetic mutations useful for evolution occur and are passed on by the generation of new individuals (reproduction) only. Genetic mutations are indeed of two types: *hereditary mutations*, which occur in the DNA contained in germ cells (egg or sperm cell) before fertilization or in the fertilized cell shortly after fertilization, so that the mutated DNA is passed on to all the organism's cells produced by the subsequent divisions of the first cell; *somatic mutations*, which occur during an organism's life in the DNA of somatic cells (cells other than germ cells), so that they are not passed on to the offspring.

Life resources (food, water, oxygen, space, and so on) are limited. A species' evolution is the primary tool for its survival and it is most efficient when parent individuals give way to the new generation, once this is able to independently provide for itself.

The rejection of decay and death by the individual who identifies as their organism is just another manifestation of the conflict between spirit and body. The spirit conceives for itself only eternity, that is, existence without start nor end, while organic life is temporary, it starts and ends.

The rejection of death in the form of fear, depression, or obsessive pursuit of physical immortality is widespread in contemporary Western society and in communisms, where materialism is rampant, but it is not and was not for most other civilizations. Most of the heroic deeds we read about in history books (or forgotten) were performed by men and women who believed in or hoped for existence after the body's death. We all enjoy daily the fruits of their actions and sacrifices.

Contemporary "cultural" production celebrates anti-heroic figures filled with "human" weaknesses such as anxiety, selfishness, opportunism, misanthropy, mental and physical illness, alcoholism, and drug addiction, in an attempt to bring the "new hero" closer to the average person. Moral mediocrity is the new normal. There is no *aspiration* to higher standards. If promoting exceptional role models in the past still left room for degradation, what is to be expected from cheap role models?

The "you only live once" cliché has risen to dogma with which one justifies any action they are ashamed of. The fact of the matter is that materialism is a trite argument: progressivism today resides in the Search for Truth and in honesty.

There are several phenomena that, as shareable and investigable experiences, would prove that the spirit's existence is not tied to the body's. There are many cases of children who tell in detail about their previous lives and of out-of-body experiences reported by people revived after an accident. Such phenomena should be a priority object of Subject Research. The fact that they are not, that they are not covered by the media, and that research carried out on them by recent-past therapists is ignored is an indication that materialism is the instrument for preserving the *status* quo: even if it turned out, as a result of

Research, that they are hallucinations or lies in the totality of cases, there is no other explanation for the current lack of interest in the subject.

Materialism makes people malleable, fearful, selfish, consumerist, supine, short-sighted, ignorant, poor, inept, enslaved. Spirituality makes the Individual independent, critical, brave, determined, strong, wise, free.

Subject and Object Research do not seem to go necessarily hand in hand. Besides, the idea that a being does not know *themselves* sounds intuitively quite contradictory. On the contrary, they should initially not know that which is other than the *self*, namely the Object, including the body as part of the physical Universe, so that a human civilization takes thousands of years to advance from mud huts to space bases and a child needs several months to learn basic information about their environment. Perhaps such an idea is simply false?

It seems more reasonable to think that the Individual knows themselves, in the depths of their consciousness. This is the premise of Socratic dialogue, whereby the philosopher made knowledge emerge in the interlocutor through questions, Eastern meditation, and hypnotism. So it is possible that Man in the past had better knowledge of the Subject than it does today, in spite of technological inferiority. If you visit an ethnological museum or read classical or ancient works, you realize that basic individual needs have never changed in space and time; they have always been the object of human attention, so that previous Research may have already found answers that went lost later.

If the Subject and the Object coincided or the former was the creator of the latter, the Subject would have to know the Object from the beginning, so that knowledge about the Object could arise from Subject Research.

$$\frac{\bullet}{=}$$

DEFENSE

War is disapproved of by most individuals. Nevertheless, it recurs over time and moves through space, with no break for Humanity.

War causes physical and spiritual suffering in all parties involved. Self-alienation is such as to open the door to the worst immorality: rape, unnecessary violence, torture, drugs. War lowers Man toward the animal state and it seems to have a constant degrading effect. It is well known that, even in peacetime, military service is often the first occasion for the individual's contact with prostitution and drug use. It probably represents the most feared event for Man, although he is the cause of it.

War causes *loss of knowledge*. It destroys monuments, works of art, and libraries, it erases ethnicities, traditions, and languages, it extinguishes philosophies and religions, it ends research and currents of thought, it kills scientists and men of letters. In a world of relative values, where right and wrong are distributed between parties with minimal spread, winners mostly portray themselves as absolute justice, altering the historiography of events and discrediting and consigning to oblivion the enemy and their culture.

The tools for preventing war are fairness, communication, and understanding. As with any interpersonal relationship, when respect is given and demanded, communication is direct, and differences of opinion are tolerated, the chances of conflict diminish dramatically, if parties act in good faith.

If we assumed complete direct communication between two non-insane individuals, where each could understand the origin of all of the other's points of view, the likelihood of disagreement would be virtually zero. If one were to place two non-insane individuals, with diametrically opposite opinions, in front of each other and instantly give them access to every piece of information, thought, experience, emotion, and reasoning pattern produced or accumulated by the other during their existence, their understanding of the other party's arguments would be nearly total. The only remaining differences would be due to each one's different and unique personality and would be easily overcome with the tiniest bit of tolerance. Agreement or compromise would be inevitable.

For example, assume allowing total communication between a non-insane American soldier and a non-insane Muslim fundamentalist. The American soldier acquires the memories of death and suffering caused by bombing, Muslim education from birth, fundamentalist indoctrination, accurate information about Western oil companies' economic interests and maneuvers in the Middle East, the lies spread about Americans, the wrongs committed by Americans, and *every* experience lived and thought produced. The Muslim fundamentalist acquires Christian education from birth, military indoctrination, enlistment propaganda, American TV reports on Middle East conflicts, the freedom principles promoted by the Founding Fathers, the lies about Muslims, the wrongs committed by Muslims, and *every* experience lived and thought produced. At the end of the process, the two would in fact be entirely new persons and would most deeply understand each other's essence. They would probably be *best friends*. A machine for instant total communication does not exist, but if enough time were devoted to communication, the outcome would be "miraculous".

Sometimes one has to deal with *insane* (i.e. destructive) individuals or nations led by them. The typical feature of these individuals is that they consider their fellow man as a threat, regardless of how well meaning or harmless the latter actually is. It seems that the two types of individual, sane and insane, find it hard to conceive of the existence of the other. An insane individual believes that others regard them as an enemy, a sane individual is incredulous in the face of evil, so much so that they try, sometimes obsessively, to find "rational" justifications for what they observe.

The origin of insanity must be addressed by Subject Research in order to identify, prevent, and cure or isolate it. This process must not result in a witch hunt: human rights remain inviolable.

Based on empirical observation, it seems that there is a recurring causal factor for many of the most vicious criminals: *overwhelm*. Serial killers, bloodthirsty dictators, pedophiles, and violent mobsters often lived overwhelming experiences at a young age. By definition, overwhelm completely overcomes the victim's reaction and it therefore depends as much on the strength of the attack as on the individual's ability to resist. Thus, the first method of preventing insanity, at least in its most brutal manifestations, is to ensure a tolerable environment for the new generations.

When one society is led by the insane, it becomes a *real* threat to the others. In this world, which is far from being peaceful, a (relatively) sane society must prepare against attacks from insane societies, in order to survive.

Although most of the population may be individually sane in a country ruled by the insane, the latter can influence their behavior through propaganda and overwhelming experiences, so

that the sane adopt destructive conduct or become insane themselves and the nation can be considered insane as a whole. It is
clear that, once the insane are dismissed, society can heal, provided that propaganda and negative experiences have not sunk
too deep roots into the individuals' minds.

When a conflict with an insane society is on the horizon,
one's communication must be aimed directly or indirectly at the
generally sane individuals in that society, so that they demand a
change in the system they belong to. This is how the USSR
came to an end: Western society offered an example of freedom,
rights, and welfare that Eastern European peoples could only
prefer to communist society's dictatorship and hardship.

Incidentally, Western society today is in danger of losing its
role as a model for others. A stagnant economy, pretended production, pseudo-democracies, lobby-controlled news, and the
privatization of basic services outline a declining trend, which
may give way to other societies. A part of Western society is still
guarding the values that accompanied its rise, but that may not
be enough to prevent legally and philosophically less advanced
societies from taking over, as it happened to countless great civilizations of the past.

A sane society must be ready for any eventuality in con-
fronting an insane nation. The regression of Humanity is an
event that no sane society as such can accept. Thus it must prepare the necessary defensive systems.

It is clear that weapons of mass destruction, including nuclear
and biological weapons, should be unanimously banned from
Earth conflicts. Accepting possession by some nations of
weapons that are capable of causing Man's extinction relatively
easily is completely irrational: from the human species' viewpoint, victory by an insane or regressive society is logically

preferable to all societies' death.

Possession of nuclear weapons is the most sensitive international issue, so much so that the International Court of Justice has held that it cannot rule on the legality of their use. It represents the fulcrum of global geopolitical balance, and the reason is simple: the *law of the strongest*. Any competition (economic, ideological, etc.) can be exacerbated to a final stage of total conflict, so that the ultimate winner of any rivalry is invariably the one who can strike the hardest. This mechanism distinguishes the international order from national ones.

Most countries live under a more or less accomplished rule of law, where law and its enforcement are imposed (more or less) equally on all individuals. The law of the strongest is suppressed by the huge apparatus (justice, law enforcement, armed forces) which the individual would collide with if they refused to comply with the system's decisions, so that judicial conflict is normally the last to occur. If the individual wished to escalate the confrontation, they would have to fight against the entire system, thus, in effect, starting a revolution.

The international order in its current state is far from representing the rule of law. Nations sign treaties and then do not ratify them, or they ratify them and then cancel them after a few years. The UN has become a bureaucratic abnormality with little influence on international affairs. The UN Security Council system established by the UN Charter, signed in 1945, was never implemented. Article 24 of the Charter states that UN Members confer responsibility for the maintenance of international peace on the Security Council, which acts on their behalf. Article 27 stipulates that all decisions by the Council on matters other than procedure are made by unanimity of the Council Permanent Members (China, France, the United Kingdom, Russia, and the

United States, i.e. the top five countries by number of nuclear warheads), so that decisions on the use of force must be approved by all Permanent Members. Article 43 stipulates that UN Members shall make available to the Security Council, through a special agreement or agreements *to be negotiated as soon as possible*, the armed forces necessary for the performance of the peacekeeping task. Article 47 stipulates the establishment of a Military Staff Committee charged with managing said armed forces' operations. In reality, peacekeeping initiatives are undertaken by individual nations or alliances, particularly NATO. The agreements mentioned in Article 43 have never been concluded and thus the Military Staff Committee has never had reason to come into existence.

The international order is a state of *nature*, where the law of the strongest rules. This is why the yearly American defense spending is greater than Saudi Arabia's GDP and Russia has sacrificed its economy for a century to maintain military means that could stand against it. For the same reason, international alliances are crucial.

International law exists and consists of customs and treaties signed by states, but it lacks an enforcement tool. This would be easily available if all nations belonged to a single rule-of-law system, but establishing an Earth federation is not advisable at present. The risks of it would be potentially fatal, similar to but worse than those of monarchy: a good government could be succeeded by terrible ones, from which though there would be no escape.

Diversity is a precious resource for survival and Progress. An Earth federation may be viable when Man has colonized other celestial bodies or portions of space. Diversity will have to be substantial, not limited to a few national entities. The best systems will necessarily prosper, the worst will decline and be subject to emigration until they change.

Solidarity and communication between individuals and between nations remain essential values. Society must be elastic: guardian of its diversity, united against common adversity. Alliance is the practical method of international law enforcement against insane nations.

THE SECOND COLD WAR

Although little media attention has been given to it, at the time of this writing we are in the midst of a Second Cold War, assuming the first one actually ended. It represents the most serious danger for life on Earth.

Three months after the attack on the World Trade Center, on December 13, 2001, the United States notified Russia of the termination of the ABM Treaty, justifying their decision with the need to protect the West from the Middle East threat. That was an agreement signed in 1972 prohibiting the two countries from making missiles that could intercept ballistic missiles (anti-ballistic missiles), so that in the event of nuclear escalation neither side could defend itself against attacks by the other. It belonged within the framework of the Mutual Assured Destruction (MAD) doctrine, for which the devastating consequences of a nuclear conflict for both sides would act as a deterrent for a first strike.

As a result, the United States started the installation of two anti-missile bases in Eastern Europe under the NATO flag: in Romania (opened in 2016) and Poland. Russia, feeling threatened by the move, reportedly responded by transferring missiles for nuclear warheads into the exclave of Kaliningrad, on the Baltic Sea. Meanwhile, Moscow invested in modernizing its nuclear arsenal and in late 2005 declared that innovations to its strategic (i.e. long-range) weapons would allow penetration of any defense system. Russia's exclusion from the G8, the war in Ukraine, and the Syrian crisis, where the U.S. and Russia support opposing sides, have definitively torn relations apart.

In the current international order, no party is willing to give up its most powerful weapons. The immediate approach to the nuclear issue should be, first and foremost, to reduce the global nuclear arsenal below the thresholds of Earth extinction and uninhabitability.

None of the nuclear-weapon states participated in the negotiation of the Treaty on the Prohibition of Nuclear Weapons, which opened for signatures in 2017, let alone signed it. The 1996 Comprehensive Nuclear Test Ban Treaty has not yet come into force because North Korea, India, and Pakistan have not signed it, and China, Egypt, Iran, Israel, and the United States have not ratified it. The speed at which disarmament will take place depends on individuals, groups, and nations' commitment to promoting the cause, which seems to have become secondary over the past two decades.

According to available information, China's nuclear arsenal would amount to approximately 300 nuclear warheads, while the United States has about 6,000 (of which 1,700 are deployed). China's military spending is equal to just over a third of the U.S.', but it has nearly *tripled* in the past ten years.

Allowing relations between the West and Russia to deteriorate is a fatal mistake. The latter, especially after abandoning communism, is culturally much closer to Europe than it is to China, just as it had been before 1917. With a nuclear arsenal virtually matching that of the U.S., Russia determines the world geopolitical balance as a potential ally for Western military supremacy or alongside the Chinese for a soon-to-be equal confrontation between the two blocs. The fact that a part of the American and European establishment pursues Russia's estrangement, rather than its inclusion, is indicative of their insanity.

After the USSR's collapse, during the last decade of the twentieth century, both the Russian government and population opened up again to Western economy and culture. The termination of the ABM Treaty marked the beginning of a regression to closure and hostility.

Conflict between nations seems to be a constant in human history, which will be overcome when Man realizes that nations are made of individuals and that governments and parliaments' only function is to represent their will, and this function is fulfilled. The fact that the only country governed by direct democracy is also the neutral one *par excellence* confirms it.

ECONOMY AND DEFENSE

Military superiority comes directly from economic superiority. Although the USSR withstood decades of Cold War, its final collapse proved that the Soviet system was not sustainable. To-day, it is clear that China is the United States' main competitor for the economic lead and, as such, it could become its main competitor for the military lead too.

The confrontation between the two countries shows all the shortcomings of capitalism, whose only goal is personal profit, even at the expense of the nation's welfare and very survival. In recent decades, China has been the destination of huge *off-shoring* of Western production. Most of the non-perishable goods being consumed in Europe and North America are pro-duced there.

First of all, as a transfer of production to an economic system outside the original one, production offshoring adds to the afore-mentioned factors that make the population poorer. By decreasing the demand for labor in the original system, it causes a decrease in the utility of the production input of the individuals belonging to it and thus in the equivalent utility these are paid with, if not actual unemployment.

Although increasing production in a less developed region is undoubtedly beneficial to human society as a whole, there is no reason to reduce production in the original system. From a na-tional point of view, offshoring makes sense when it is balanced by the emergence of new types of work and jobs in the original system and it is accompanied by the training of workers in the new tasks. In reality, it is mostly done for the profit of private actors only, as evidenced by unemployment rates in Western countries.

Governments should implement intervention policies to dis-courage it, for example by applying special taxes that neutralize labor savings pursued by companies through offshoring. They should support companies within their borders so that they are not encouraged or even forced to offshore, first and foremost by ensuring rational and tolerable taxation.

Offshoring towards jurisdictions that are antithetical to one's own is doubly dangerous. A nation allowing itself to it gets poorer, while it makes a potential enemy richer and it makes itself *dependent* on them. As much as Western society is intoxicated with finance and digitization, organisms' basic needs are way more concrete: water, food, clothing, shelter, transportation, and energy. While the West juggles stocks, bonds, derivatives, and futures, production of *real* goods keeps flowing out to the East, soon irremediably. "Pieces of paper" have an agreed value only, which in the event of a conflict is ignored in the blink of an eye. Depriving oneself of the means of real production to the advantage of non-liberal jurisdictions is a suicidal act.

Offshoring often results in hypocrisy: while worker rights are loudly advocated at home, goods produced mostly by those who do not enjoy them are consumed.

THE ARMED FORCES

The armed forces and law enforcement fulfill the *mission* of defending their nation's values. Their members must be *models* of justice and ethics. They must treat the individuals they protect with the same respect that is due to them.

The ideological structure of armies must be reformed, replacing obedience with *understanding*. Imposition of blind obedience normally conceals irrational and destructive intentions, otherwise it would not be necessary: the fact that it represents a cornerstone of military discipline confirms war's irrationality.

Hierarchy must reflect the logic of distribution of functions and the use of urgent orders, such that they do not allow evaluation by the executor, would be limited to exceptional emergency cases where the value of immediate action outweighs that of individual judgment. Although it is sometimes perceived as or realized in the abuse by an individual of another, hierarchy should actually be understood simply as efficient division of tasks: the task of deciding and that of executing. Those in higher positions must have the ability to make decisions, thanks to their natural ability and the expertise they acquired in previous decision-making or executive functions. The executor is not deprived of the ability to make decisions when executing an order: after all, he or she is responsible for every action he or she performs, regardless of whether it stems from another's order. At the same time, the executor understands the value of hierarchy and urgency in their decision to fulfill the order. This *understanding* comes from the education provided to the individual on the value and purpose of their function and on the organizational system they participate in.

In the pursuit of Individual Sovereignty, the obsolete concept of authoritarian hierarchy, in all human groups, is thus replaced with *functional organization*. Democracy is a step toward political individual sovereignty, i.e. in the realm of decisions of general concern. At the administrative level, it is inefficient to consult the entire staff on every issue, and the campaigning effort required to convince people of a choice's value, which is typical of democracy, would not be sustainable. So the validity of an order comes from the principle of division of functions, not from the superiority of one individual over another. Just as no country is called upon to submit to another, by virtue of the principle of national sovereignty, so no individual should be subject to another, under any circumstances, by virtue of the pursuit of Individual Sovereignty.

Orders must be subject to the executor's power to request their review, if reasonable grounds exist. For this principle to be applied at all times, any automated armed unit (drone, robot, or similar) must be controlled by one individual. National legal systems and international law must not allow multiple military or police automated units to be led by one individual. That would represent a direct threat to democracy and peace. Responsibility for forceful acts must remain distributed.

Communication and interactions between individuals in an organization are held at an equal level, without any paternalism. Mutual respect as individuals is an essential right and duty. Esteem and, when it's the case, reverence are aroused in others by one's conduct and achievements, not by title. True *leaders* are so by virtue of their sense of responsibility for others' welfare and their awareness of their duty to use their extraordinary ability to make things work. To prevent traditional meanings from being confused with the new system, orders can be called "decisions".

Those who see the socialist stamp on this should remember that socialism, a self-declared champion of equality and parity, has provided examples of the most elephantine and abusive hierarchical organizations in its applications: yet another proof of its deceptiveness. While socialism aims at the general *lowering* of the population, in effect subjecting it to the few, *functional organization* pursues the *elevation* of all individuals to the inherent dignity of human beings.

•
=

THE REFORMATIVE SYSTEM

What has long been called the *penitentiary* (= "penance") *system* in various jurisdictions, today should clearly have only the goal of *reformation* or, at most, *preservation.*

In a society aspiring to Individual Sovereignty, no one would have the right to administer punishments. With the exception of the depraved, human beings commit essentially the same "sins", even if they try to hide them from others for fear of harming their reputation or being punished.

Secrets are unhealthy, they burden the conscience and require lies to conceal them, which are in turn perceived as wrongdoing, thus triggering a vicious cycle of secrecy and guilt. Individuals should be free to confess any wrongdoing they have committed, without being punished. Reproof is unnecessary when the individual is already aware of their responsibility. This does not exclude the private or criminal consequences of the harm caused, nor does it amount to publicly telling about everyone's business or targeting the population with negative news: the prevailing practice by contemporary media.

Guilt has no utility. Allowing oneself to it and withdrawing from life, out of self-contempt or fear of hurting someone again, is in itself wrongdoing. A peculiar trait of the insane is that they do not feel guilt. They regard others as threats: weakening them is a reasonable act. On closer inspection, this represents an advantage for them, since no remorse slows them down or distracts them from their goals.

It is the sane individual's duty, for their own and others' welfare, to prevent guilt from lowering their energy, confidence, and determination in pursuing social and individual progress. Failing in this duty opens the door to the regression pursued by the insane. Guilt must turn into *responsibility*, accepting authorship of one's acts and continuing one's positive efforts.

No sane individual makes a mistake believing it to be so when making it. It is always an attempt to achieve more good than harm. The individual who cheats on their partner or steals, takes drugs, and so on, believes in that instant to derive value (physical, emotional, "spiritual" pleasure) from it that is greater than the disvalue it produces (loss of trust, physical health, etc.), otherwise they would not do it. At most, such an individual can be blamed for an incorrect balancing of values, resulting from their awareness, willpower, education, environmental influences, experiences, and IQ. It is clear that sane inmates, probably being the majority of the prison population, have not committed their crimes out of pure evil.

The reformation of inmates is pursued through a journey that supports and stimulates their individual critical analysis of their upbringing, environmental influences, and negative experiences. How can disobedience to rules be imputed to a thief raised by parents who taught them to steal? The individual is, in fact, obeying the first rules they learnt: those from parent education.

Of course, the individual's willingness to improve their condition is a prerequisite for any reformative process. The insane normally have no sincere intention to change their conduct; they believe they are totally right. The sane are typically inclined to embark on any constructive activity unless they have a considerable distrust of their environment due to previous negative experiences, which can anyway be overcome by reformation. In any case, no one can be forcibly subjected to psychological, religious, medical, or similar practices.

A reformation program should first include basic education on society's rules and functioning, offering rational viewpoints which the reformee can critically compare to those acquired during their existence. Vocational courses should be offered to inmates in order to facilitate their social reintegration. Inmates should be employed for at least eight hours a day to meet the costs of incarceration. Any surplus produced by an inmate should be compensated through an incentive and bonus system allowing them better material and spiritual conditions. Those who refuse work should enjoy only basic support in the name of the principle of social solidarity, anyway without exemption from the economic debt that follows.

FAMILY

Family is a fundamental form of aggregation of individuals in society. Its importance is due to its function of objectifying the love between two people and educating offspring.

Family provides for and protects new individuals until they are autonomous. In the current social system, family is normally the form of closest solidarity among its members. The bond it is founded on derives spiritually from: the love between the parents; the parents' love for their children; the sharing of goals and values achieved by living together, communication, and education; the children's grateful love toward their parents. The family bond is also physically based on: the physical attraction between the parents; the reproduction instinct (perpetuation of the species); the instinct to perpetuate one's genetic heritage ("blood bond").

Family is another manifestation of the coexistence of spirit and body. The family bond is spiritual and physical and cannot go without the two components. Very deep bonds may come into existence in other forms, but none of them is a *family* bond, according to the definition of family considered here. Monogamy, as a social and individual value, may come from the need to preserve such bond and thus protect family as an incubator of new individuals.

Taking family apart leads to very large gaps in the development of a new society member, as it affects: material and spiritual support; material and spiritual protection; the learning of personal, family (for the formation of a future new family), and social (moral and legal rules) values; the learning of basic knowledge (awareness of self and the environment); the learning of elementary individual (including reading, writing, and calculation) and social (communication, manners, customs) skills.

The physical characteristics of men and women have traditionally produced function differentiation. In today's average human state, where the individual is unable to leave the materiality of their existence, ignoring the differences between the two sexes in the name of spirit's asexuality is as noble an attempt theoretically as it is objectively foolish; doing so in a materialistic society is pharisaic.

The female body's anatomy is more fit for reproduction than the male body is, which in turn is more suitable to work, in the term's most scientific sense: force applied along a distance (in primitive life: lifting an x kg stone y meters off the ground, dragging a prey for z km, and so on). The relatively high frequency of the menstrual cycle, with its physical and mental effects on the individual, constantly influences the organism.

Progress, as an expansion of the dominion of reason over matter, has made human work gradually less physical. This has allowed the equalization of genders in many professions.

However, the equalizing trend of recent decades, heavily influenced by loud "social justice" propaganda, has ended up *unfairly* ignoring biological differences between the sexes. Many women during their period are forced to take painkillers so as not to be absent from work and not to affect their productivity, that is, to match male production. Medication should be reserved for the treatment of pathological, not *physiological*, conditions. In many countries, maternity leave is only a few months long and coincides with the average breastfeeding period only, thus forcing many women to neglect their maternal function after weaning. Here is injustice in the name of "equality".

The core of the matter does not pertain to national legislations, which at best aim at containing welfare costs, but to society's "customs" and, in particular, to the propaganda that has established them.

The materialistic drift of recent decades has produced a consumerist society where individual value is measured by the *possession* of material goods (so-called status symbols). The individual is "forced" to consume their wealth in tropical vacations to be shared on social media, designer furniture, electronic devices, tennis rackets, golf clubs, and fancy plastic bags. This and non-production and every other kind of unfair exchange have made the population poorer.

The average family today has one child, is supported by two parents, and rents an apartment or takes out a 30-year mortgage to buy one. Fifty years ago, the average family had two children, was supported by a labourer or craftsman father, and lived in a home they owned.

From this angle, the essence of economic equalization emerges and belies the apparent aspirations of equity of movements that have so easily overlooked women's necessities: in today's materialistic social system, women are *forced* to work. Women should be guaranteed the right to work as much as the right to be mothers, but even more the right to *be women*.

Materialism, understood as the identification of the self with the body, has changed the hierarchy of personal and social values, so that money and material goods are replacing any other value at its apex, including the care of children and family in general.

The equality of human and civil rights, which is the *true* recent progress of gender equalization, would not have led to the *identification* of women with men if money, a consequence of work, had not risen to be the prime value of both capitalist and communist and every other kind of society.

There are obvious biological reasons why women have traditionally been responsible for raising their own or others' children: first, their maternal instinct, shared with most of other animal species. Second, a lower testosterone level results in less muscular strength and aggressiveness compared to males, which makes the female physiologically better suited for stable cohabitation with the new individual. Although the average human being is endowed with a far higher spirit-to-body ratio than that of the other Earth species (so that one's emotions are primarily originated by the spirit), hormones, drugs, and medication are capable of influencing one's mood, to a greater or lesser degree. Testosterone also influences sexual desire and, according to FBI statistics, 96 percent of pedophiles are male.

In fact, the reason why the female body is better suited for child care is due to organisms' natural *specialization*. Diversity, again, is a fundamental resource for life, and the division of functions within any group, from family to Mankind, guarantees the necessary efficiency for its survival.

Equality between women and men is equality of rights and dignity. Claiming physical and behavioral equality is absurd, and those who advocate it are either naive or pursuing ulterior motives.

The disintegration of family unity, produced by pulling women away from their children, has terrible economic and political consequences. A child that is neglected when they are not yet autonomous may suffer physical, behavioral, emotional, mental, and spiritual shortcomings throughout their life. Each consequence has an economic cost to society: educational, health, legal, and, in the worst case, reformative costs. These must be subtracted from the value produced by working women in the social balance.

Taking new individuals away from family education and submitting them to standardized education, similarly to fascist, Nazi, and communist indoctrination, uniforms the educational content and homogenizes the educational system's output: the *standardized* individual.

Standardized educational content, being established by ministries of education, is subject to the political influence of the ruling government and is peppered with teachers' opinions. As in totalitarian dictatorships, the building of values in young individuals is appropriated by the state apparatus.

State intervention on family should be limited to ensuring a tolerable environment for the child. Society and education should be inclusive enough to offer the new individual alternative perspectives to those given daily by their parents, without defrauding the latter of their role.

LEADERSHIP

Until Individual Sovereignty is realized, it is natural for portions of the population to be spontaneously represented by leaders to some extent. Their function is to *inspire*, *serve*, and *coordinate* the group they represent. Their purpose should be social progress, that is, in current jurisdictions, the transition from totalitarianism to democracy and from indirect democracy to direct democracy.

Leaders accompany society along the path of evolution, they do not throw it into situations it is not prepared for. Converting a centuries-long dictatorship, where citizens have lost their sense of responsibility and ability to make decisions, into a direct democracy overnight would produce chaos, with short-term regressive effects.

Historical examples are countless. French Revolution was accompanied by the transition from an absolute monarchy to a short republican interlude, to Napoleon's dictatorship, to half a century of instability between restorations of monarchy and further revolutions. The difference with the earlier American Revolution lies in the leaders who took part in it and in the pre-existing administrative system. In America there was an extraordinary concentration of morally outstanding figures, in a short period of time, which ensured enlightened and stable leadership in the delicate first decades of the new state's life: the wise and determined leaders of the Revolution succeeded each other in the presidency for nearly thirty years (Washington, Adams, Jefferson, Madison). The Thirteen Colonies' constitutional systems already included elected legislative bodies.

The USSR's collapse in the 1990s was followed by a decade of very severe economic crisis accompanied by a widespread increase in crime and corruption. After nearly a century of communism, a population unused to political responsibility and private initiative was thrown into a Western-like model of indirect democracy and free markets. Thus, thirty years later, the economy is still controlled by the so-called *oligarchs*, the few entrepreneurs who took possession of the large Soviet companies during privatizations and their descendants, and political power is markedly centralized. Although harshly criticized by the Western ruling class, this system is the natural consequence of eighty years of communism and its inevitable end, along with a lack of leaders capable of inspiring, serving, and coordinating the transition at the dawn of the Russian Federation. That said, the existing cultural and ideological base plays a considerable role in the emergence and rise of good leaders.

The ideal leader has all three skills. He or she is, first and foremost, able to communicate concepts to people. This does not require a degree in literature or even loquacity. It requires a firm belief in the principles they advocate and the ability to make them understandable.

Most politicians have focused exclusively on communication, turning themselves into a bunch of salesmen with no management skills nor values, serving those who decide and administer behind the scenes. Symmetrically, a large part of the population pays attention to a politician's appearance and eloquence more than to the concepts they express and *facts*. The average citizen complains about politicians' ineffectuality, but they do not change their criteria for choosing their representatives: popular movements that stand as alternatives to traditional parties, from which the *same* type of figure constantly emerges, evidence that.

On the other hand, there are leaders who arouse dislike in part of the population because of their tone or personality, but who have proved *in fact* to pursue the common good much better than their competitors. As much as it is preferable to be led by an individual whose manner suggests balance and stability of spirit and conduct, facts are far more important than appearance and, in today's society, the ideal solution is often *very far* from the best option available at a given time.

Social and political leadership is a mission, like all public functions. It is philanthropy. Its purpose is the common good, that is, the Progress of individuals and society. It is fueled by a desire to end the suffering of honest beings and to give them the world they deserve. It is inspired by the desire to spare children from overwhelm and self-alienation and to preserve the individual essence of all. A leader makes decisions regardless of their personal interest. This is a rare talent, with which comes the responsibility to lead others. It is a deeply felt responsibility, which one cannot and does not want to escape.

History is full of people who were able to win approval, but who were motivated by a thirst for money, power, and glory rather than Progress. Sometimes it has been a mixture of good intentions and personal interest. A good leader's work deserves to be rewarded with wealth and esteem, but their decisions must be dictated only by the social Purpose. Their greatest reward is the *success* of their efforts: the satisfaction from having succeeded in their intention to help others and themselves. By definition, success proper is the achievement of a set goal; only in a broad sense it is the fame that comes from it.

A leader must be able to manage a group. They must be able to devise strategies and get them executed. They must be able to delegate power and responsibility. A good leader is a good administrator: the best ideas, without systematic planning and implementation, are rarely realized.

Identifying and training one's potential successors is an essential aspect of good organization. Progress is neither pursued nor achieved in the span of a lifetime. Planning must be far-sighted and transcend current actors. All three constituents of leadership play their roles in this trait. In fact, the leadership of one who has inspired, served, and administered well enough will survive their death.

Many of the best people set goals that were achieved after they passed away: a vision's greatness can almost be measured by the time it takes to be realized. The ability to set aside self-interest allowed them to do without their contemporaries' admiration. These individuals' "self-interest", that is, their innermost desire, is Progress for themselves and society. They are brave people, who are so certain of their convictions as not to seek others' immediate approval and to persevere in spite of their disinterest or contempt. On the other hand, thanks to the speed of communication and movement enabled by the advancement of technology, changes are much faster today than in the past.

A movement's longevity can serve as a measurement of the quality of the leadership that originated it. The longest-lived movements, which transcend geopolitics over centuries and millennia, seem to be the religious ones. Christianity, for example, has survived from the Roman Empire, through monarchies, democracies, and dictatorships, up to the American "empire". Jesus Christ, as he is described, was undoubtedly a great leader, embodying all three essential skills. Unquestionably he was able to inspire and serve his followers. His awareness was so solid as not to compromise with a hostile environment. His selflessness enabled him to give up his life for his cause. Also, he *chose* the Apostles, who would establish the Church of Jerusalem and spread the new faith to the world. Evidently, this form of organization was as simple as it was effective. Similarly, in the East, Gautama Buddha founded and regulated the Buddhist monk community, which to date has existed for two and a half millennia.

The reason why religious movements are the most deeply rooted and long-lasting lies in their Purpose: spiritual salvation or freedom. This reveals individuals' prime tendency to pursue ultra-corporeal existence. No materialistic movement seems to be able to pursue the satisfaction of a more pressing need, and no artistic, literary, or political movement equals religious ones in terms of longevity.

For materialists, religion is an illusory desire for immortality, but very few of them seem able to bear the burden of "disillusion", and many admit suffering from depression or other "mental disorders" and/or regularly take drugs, psychiatric drugs, and/or alcohol. Can Man find happiness only in illusion? Is he really doomed to a miserable existence? Is his biological evolution so flawed as to have produced a being who is a victim of his own existential reflections, whose survival capacity is compromised by his apathy or by the use of psychotropic substances, which are toxic to his own organism?

Today's *global* society is approaching an unprecedented stage in known human history where materialistic individuals, who regard themselves merely as bodies, outnumber those who have some conception of spiritual existence. This is happening under pressure from the Western materialistic drift on the one hand and Eastern communism on the other. Traditional religious movements are decaying mainly by their own fault, having themselves yielded to the materialistic influence that led them to put material wealth before the spiritual one, and to some extent due to materialistic propaganda, thus dragging the doctrines they represent into oblivion too.

For a new social movement to last long, it must have a purpose that enables it to do so, one that transcends the temporary needs of present society and pursues individuals' welfare down the ages. Such a movement must enter human history at this exact moment of transition in spirituality. Between the extremes of past dogmatic religion and potential future materialism, the middle way to self-knowledge has opened before Man, in a context of maximum development of science, technology, and law. The price of not taking *this* opportunity could be the extinction of this and other species.

Materialism weakens leadership. The great leaders of the past, conceiving an afterlife for themselves and others, more easily summoned the necessary courage for risky ventures and far-sighted goals, often antagonizing the powerful and sometimes giving up their lives.

Modern "philosophy" supports the idea that there are no *certainties*. The inability to derive certainties from observation or logical thinking is deeply incapacitating. A leader who has no convictions cannot genuinely inspire anyone, let alone serve others. They cannot be anything but a liar, as an advocate of causes they do not believe in.

RESOURCES

FINITENESS AND ETERNITY

The conflict between spirit and body causes persistent problems, which will only be finally solved when one component prevails over the other. The availability of natural resources is one of them.

Although the Universe appears to be infinite, human reality has accustomed us to materiality's finiteness. The potential infinity of space would not necessarily correspond to the infinity of matter.

Man should draw up an account of Earth's available resources, their exploitation, and their renewal. The goal would be achieving equivalence between resources obtained (or renewed) and resources used.

Another empirical conclusion about the nature of the physical Universe is the impermanence (temporariness) of conditions. Each of its entities is constantly subject to the influence of another element, force, or energy. Change never stops, eternity does not seem to be an attribute of anything but an initial amount of available energy at most.

Every natural resource, such as internal Earth heat and solar energy, is destined to end, and technological progress has the function of replacing it. Artificial renewal (recycling) of matter is not completely efficient at present, so that part of the resource is wasted.

If Man is unable to meet breakeven for his own sustenance, that is, the equivalence of cost and income in terms of resources, he will become extinct. Even if he were able to conquer the entire Universe at the expense of all competing species, resources would eventually run out, unless matter were infinite. The elimination of the other species would anyway have a very high cost in terms of compromise between spirit and body, which would be acceptable only to a species that has lost most of its spiritual component and, thus, of its sense of solidarity.

Any dominant species, in order to survive long, must take care of its ecosystem, as this sustains it. If the species at the top of the food chain were to kill too many individuals of the species feeding it, it would cause its own population to shrink until systemic balance is restored. If the same species killed *all* the individuals on which it feeds, it would become extinct.

When Man achieves resource breakeven, he will have produced a sustainable system capable of sustaining him on a lasting basis.

By analyzing reality more objectively, it is inevitable to observe the existence of factors that reduce the human species' probability of surviving forever to an infinitesimal. This is a fact and it is so obvious as it is neglected, as it conflicts with the primary instinct of every species to survive.

Nothing seems to be capable of eternity in the physical Universe. This is the essence of the conflict between spirit and body: the spirit conceives eternity and hopes for it; the soul's eternity is the premise of all religions.

Eternity is an essential attribute, not an incidental one. It does not depend on circumstances. Eternity for any entity can be excluded the moment there is at least one threat to its existence.

Mathematically, at an infinite time, even the least probable but possible event occurs. Given the cyclical nature of conditions in the Universe, however, it is probable that new life would arise at some later remote point in time, if the present one were to die.

OVERPOPULATION

The fundamental goal of all species is survival, which is qualified in terms of quality and quantity. The qualitative characteristics of survival can be identified in the degree of security, comfort, and longevity of individual existence, as determined by individual access to resources. Quantity is the number of individuals belonging to the species. Nature, as with any other process, tends toward a balance between the two values. The instinct of reproduction is second only to the instinct of individual survival in animals, and sometimes it even prevails over the latter. When there is plenty of resources, neo-individuals are more likely to survive and there is an increase in the species population. If the increase is excessive, so that resources are not sufficient to sustain all individuals, the weakest among them perish and the population shrinks. Thus, each species naturally tends toward an effective trade-off between quality and quantity of its own survival.

Population growth naturally pursued by all species leads them to expand their environment. As Humankind and other species extend their scope to new planets, planetary systems, and galaxies, they will necessarily end up meeting or colliding

with each other. Like on Earth, civilizations that are less spiritually evolved than others may prevail.

Human reason tends to pursue balance before nature runs its course, in an effort to save resources and spare individuals suffering. Consequently, various theories have been put forth about Earth overpopulation and limiting population growth. First, it is necessary to ascertain their scientific foundations, especially mathematical ones, in the light of an accurate resource inventory. Second, their origin as well as any of their authors' own interests must be verified.

Quality and quantity are both essential to a species' survival. Limiting quantity for quality can have disastrous effects. Reality proves that a species, civilization, race, nation, company, or group that is larger than another is more likely to prevail.

The minimum quality level pursued by said theories should be ascertained: in a consumerist society, it could be set well above that of the most efficient compromise between quality and quantity.

Reproduction, as the only means of genetic mutation, allows biological diversification. A reduction of the reproduction rate would slow down a species' evolution.

Some of these theories argue that the level of individual health would be inversely proportional to the population growth rate of a human group, so that an improvement in individual health would correspond to a slowdown in growth. Thus they regard *health care* as a means of countering overpopulation. The rationale would lie in the fact that if individuals' probability of survival increased, the need for excess reproduction would end. For example: if a couple considered a total number of three children as ideal (in terms of support in old age, contribution to the species, or any other consideration), they would have to generate six new individuals, in an environment where the probability of survival up to adulthood is 50 percent; if that probability increased to 75 percent, they would have to generate only four.

On closer inspection, this is a deceptive argument. In fact, population growth *is produced* by the improvement of individual health, without which new individuals would not have the chance to survive and thus constitute such growth. The actual intentions of those who use "health care" for population control should be thoroughly investigated. The pursuit of criminal intentions behind a veneer of solidarity is a typical and insidious expedient used by insane individuals to gain public approval.

The slowdown or even the end of population growth is caused by a change in the social paradigm, that is, a change in the *values* of a human group. A materialistic and consumerist society tends to prioritize available individual *material quality*, firstly for oneself and secondly for one's offspring, over *quantity* (number of individuals). This is the trend embraced by Western society, which may cause it to be defeated by societies devoted to more traditional values, unless it turns into a *global trend*.

Even from a materialistic viewpoint, whereby one only lives once and only as a body, denying another the pleasure of existence in order to afford a tablet, a bigger car, or finer furniture sounds extremely selfish; actually to an even greater extent than from a religious perspective, whereby life is not limited to (one) bodily existence. It would also be in utter contradiction with the materialistic obstinacy to sustain severely disabled individuals who are *not* able to enjoy the pleasure of existence, that is, to perceive, communicate, and move. Materialism, like any other form of excess, is deceptive, unbalanced, and inconsistent.

THE WAY OUT

Inter-species competition, necessary population growth, and in general the cyclical nature of the Universe and its parts reveal a harsh truth: there is no material solution to the human problem of resources, nor to any other conflict between spirit and body, for any living species. Even if Man achieved perfect resource renewability, purposely limited his expansion, and persuaded every other species to do the same, life as a whole would still be subject to cosmic events, such as the cooling of planets, the depletion of stars, and so on.

There is only an infinite number of *compromises* sustaining life, between *two final outcomes*: the *material* one, where life becomes extinct and every organism goes back to the state of inanimate matter, and the *spiritual* one, where individuals exist as spirit, free from the constraints of matter. In both cases, there will be a separation between spirit and body and the end of *living beings*. The difference will lie in the way the separation will take place (forced and passive in the first case, intentional and active in the second) and in the spirit's condition. In the second case, the spirit will have realized its potential to the point of rising above matter; in the first case, the spirit may be at least defeated, if not nearly unconscious, if the materialistic drift has been so deep as to make them identify with their body and consider themselves "dead" upon its death.

The only way a human being can survive happily without clouding their consciousness with alcohol, drugs, psychiatric drugs, or other means seems to be the hope, however little and concealed, of existing eternally in some form. Even a happy materialist, provided they exist, harbors an albeit remote hope of eternal survival as a body. Even a happy and altruistic materialist, provided they exist, hopes for their species' eternity. Even a happy and far-sighted materialist, if they existed, would hope for life's eternity in the Universe.

Against the above view it could be argued that the conflicts being described are not about spirit and body, but they are internal to material existence. From that perspective, conflicting desires would serve to pursue the best compromise for survival. For example, the conflict between hunger and reluctance to kill an animal would lead the individual to kill only when strictly necessary, so as not to destroy one's ecosystem and to achieve the most efficient resource allocation. Also, the conflict between sex drive and the sense of marital fidelity could make the individual choose the best-suiting partner for reproduction and the development and care of a family.

However, Man's "awareness" of such a state of affairs, where dissatisfaction and pain are inherent to existence and inescapable, where there is no hope of eternity, makes him unhappy, less active, and immoral, thus reducing his ability to survive and neutralizing any possible utility of inner conflicts.

Man, like any other individual or society, is lost without the Purpose. Knowing that his material component is surely destined to end deprives him of any earthly purpose worthy of his intelligence and it reveals to him the only viable path: that of the spirit. Whenever he pursues a different purpose from the one inherent to him, such as limited or partial purposes, he produces alterations in his evolution and gets completely lost upon its attainment. Past civilizations proved this: by pursuing territorial expansion, glory, and material power, they died out after success. The greatest empires on Earth collapsed upon themselves despite their overwhelming advantage over any external rival.

In Western society, the individual goal is *wealth* and the signs of its attainment appear: individuals who are bored, addicted to narcotics, selfish, disoriented, manic, depressed, apathetic, unhappy. Barring a sudden change, Western society's fate is clear. Any activity *ends* upon reaching its purpose.

Individuals' natural Purpose is the highest degree of welfare, in qualitative terms of *happiness, freedom, ability,* and *knowledge,* and in quantitative terms of *longevity.* The individual, upon achievement of the Purpose, would bear the traits of what has traditionally been defined as *God*: an *omnipotent* and *eternal* being. The Purpose cannot be achieved by the body. While eternity has been "granted" to every soul by traditional religions, omnipotence remained an attribute of the god or gods to which individuals would be subject. Once religious monarchy or oligarchy is overcome and individual spiritual sovereignty is established, the individual's *essence* is acknowledged, so that the pursuit of the Purpose is in fact a return to the state of Self.

III

THE CURRENT SCENE

AN ANATOMY OF DEMOCRACY

As seen above, consensus in a democratic society is the cornerstone of political power. As long as there is a majority of opinion, the democratic system works. The goal of winning consensus has led to the propaganda battles between lobbies that have characterized society since Western monarchies were removed from power.

In an ideal democracy, society would be made up in its entirety of mentally healthy individuals, who, as such, would share the *purpose* of general welfare. Individuals would be endowed with such knowledge and reason that they would even agree on the *ways* to achieve it, with minimal compromise. In fact, this would represent the last stage of democracy, i.e. its end, when individuals would be so rational and skillful that they could govern themselves: Individual Sovereignty.

In practice, there are some insane individuals (let us call them "wolves") who do not share the purpose of common welfare, because they consider others to be a threat. There are some definitely sane individuals (the "shepherds") who actively support the purpose, because they consider others as beings worthy of respect and as assets. The rest of the population (the "herd") tends to be sane, but it is subject to direction by others and by their present personal interests. The image an individual offers of themselves does not necessarily correspond to their innermost tendencies, so that you run across wolves disguised as sheep or even shepherds.

There are insane beings with high intelligence and excellent knowledge of the system, who use these to increase their power and subject others. This is the case with well-trained politicians who consistently make wrong decisions or make gross "mistakes", such as an economist raising taxes during a recession, whose conduct is simply malicious. There are generally sane beings with little education or critical thinking.

The only tool the insane have, in a democratic system, to make up for being fewer is propaganda through the media, culture, and education, whose effectiveness derives from the original lack of knowledge and/or intelligence in the public.

There are mainly three solutions that have been promoted throughout history to remedy the weaknesses of democracy, two of which are regressive. One is a return to monarchy, whose ruler can be called anything — king, dictator, emperor — but the essence is that one individual has unconditional power over others. This is what happened in Rome in 44 B.C., when the Senate proclaimed a perpetual dictatorship. This solution might produce exceptional results for at most a few decades, if the new monarch were a sane and wise person, but it would undermine the system in the long run, first by raising the issue of succession. If it were an "elective monarchy", i.e. the population exercised its power of choice only for the election of a new monarch to whom sovereignty would be returned, it would allow the opportunity for insane individuals to grab totalitarian power through propaganda. This would be facilitated by the fact that the population, by exercising sovereignty only occasionally, would lose interest in politics and thus knowledge and judgment on political issues.

The most important reason why a return to monarchy (or oligarchy) is not a viable solution is that it does not aim at an increase of individual capacity and responsibility and thus at Progress, but it rather moves in the opposite direction. It is like a parent who does not allow their child to grow up. The individual who is offered the office of monarch, if they are a true leader, would reject it, as they would be aware of causing regression. The impossibility that a new monarch could be such a gifted leader as to justify a return to monarchy is thus logically demonstrated.

The second "solution" is a ban on propaganda. This is a violation of the fundamental freedom of expression and should be abhorred as such.

The only solution, the most laborious but the only effective one, is individual growth. Through Subject and Object Research and education aimed at the development of critical and independent individual thinking, free from propaganda influence, a *competent* voter base is produced and, through generations, consolidates to the point of being impregnable to any regressive propaganda initiative.

THE DICHOTOMY DECEPTION

Propaganda, in a neutral sense of promoting ideas or movements, is the most common way of influencing consensus around the social purpose and the means to achieve it. It can take place as overt support for theories or goals or as covert dissemination of these through newspapers, television, radio, web, film, literature, music, art in general, education, and so on.

When the general interest conflicts with that of a powerful few (and their entourage), these may seek to influence consensus through propaganda, like any other political player. Its intensity will depend on the availability of financial resources and media. It would apparently promote causes that are beneficial to the community, while concealing the pursuit of their own interests.

Propaganda, as a tool available more or less to all lobbies, does not ensure the winning of consensus. Especially in the era of global free communication, the Internet, and social media (provided they are not subject to censorship), money and control of the press do not guarantee a campaign's success. Moreover, the population, repeatedly disappointed by broken promises, has developed a skeptical and rejecting attitude toward direct propaganda and quite some disinterest in, as well as disillusion with, politics.

When playing a game, there is always a chance of losing, regardless of how superior one's means are compared to the opponent's. In order to completely rule out defeat, there are only two logically viable ways: (1) not to play; (2) to be all players at the same time, i.e. to play against oneself.

The application of (1) in democracy is to deprive consensus of its fundamental role, that is, to avoid the game of winning consensus, which is the democratic game itself. The way to do this is to make political parties divide up the electorate in equivalent shares. One limits individuals' knowledge and reason and fuels rivalries to ensure disagreement within the population over the social purpose to be pursued and the means to do so. It is the *divide-and-rule* strategy — while two dogs are fighting for a bone, a third one runs away with it.

Instrumentalized politicians, instead of discussing compromises to avoid disastrous stalemates in the management of the state, take part in TV fights and oppose any initiative promoted by the other side to the bitter end, thus utterly spoiling their mission as public officials serving the community.

The population is split into two opposing sides, like sports fans, without realizing that they belong to the same team and admitting that there are positive ideas and values on both sides. A kind of political insanity is produced, where people regard the other side only as a threat rather than an asset.

This scene, which all Western democracies facing governability issues for lack of solid majorities can be identified with, opens the door to lobbies' intervention, technocratic governments, and all other forms of *non-democratic* external interference. Some even feel justified in saying that democracy does not work.

The second way to escape the democratic game is to represent all sides in the game. Regardless of who wins, your goals would be pursued in any case.

A private power can secure the services of members of all major parties, so that the election outcome is essentially irrelevant.

In some countries, politicians as a social class have become so consolidated and isolated from the population as to constitute a lobby themselves, pursuing their own class interests. Here the "parties" stage a clash, but behind the scenes they go hand in hand.

Both expedients are necessarily onerous. In order to maximize their efficiency, one must first reduce the amount of players to the minimum possible number: two. This facilitates both the splitting of consensus and control over the parties. Thus we end up with Right versus Left, North versus South, Republicans versus Democrats, Conservatives versus Labour, Capitalists versus Socialists, Fascists versus Communists. These are convenient, artificial, and arbitrary dichotomies, which do not even remotely represent the infinite variability of both human thought and reality. They are tools of people *control*.

A rigid two-party system is *not* democracy. Forcing all political beliefs to converge into two groupings and submit to their internal power dynamics is *not* free choice of one's representatives.

As a demonstration of such dualisms' deceptiveness, the level of contradiction is so high that the average voter is not even able to understand which principles one and the other group identify with. Investment banks and multinational corporations, the same ones that embody the worst side of capitalism, support left and liberal parties. Former socialists and communists lead right-wing parties. Historically libertarian figures support technocrats.

Communism and extreme capitalism are regressive ideologies that lead to the same result: subjecting society to few individuals. The second, by openly setting the goal of *personal material wealth* (quite different from the Purpose of *individual wellbeing*) at the expense of other values, justifies ruthless and oppressive conduct. The first pursues the same goal, but in a hidden way.

Although surprisingly often ignored by schoolbooks, it is a historically known fact that the first communist experience in the contemporary age (the Soviet one) is the result of a German attempt to destabilize Russia. It was indeed the German Empire that allowed the repatriation of the exiled Lenin and financed his party and propaganda.

Incidentally, the two main communist revolutions (the Russian one in October 1917 and the Chinese one in 1946) did not remove monarchies (the tzar in Russia and the imperial dynasty in China), but rather replaced governments that were already republican: the Russian Republic, established seven months earlier with the February Revolution, and the Republic of China, born after the 1911 Revolution. In both cases, communists took advantage of a time of systemic weakness in their respective countries: the recent republican revolution in Russia, and the post-war crisis after the Sino-Japanese War.

Communism preaches sharing and distribution, while its applications, from Latin America to Asia, have achieved the most impressive *centralizations*, accompanied by idolatry and cult of personality.

If capitalism can enrich one class and impoverish many people, communism impoverishes all. Preferring the suffering of an entire nation to that of a portion of it, even if it is a majority portion, is in fact biologically illogical and insane.

Communism is the fruit of petty feelings of envy. Its motto is "Misery loves company". Those who eagerly promote it are driven by a thirst for wealth and power, which they seek to take from others through the deception of their ideology. If they cannot enjoy that wealth so as not to reveal their fraud, they prefer to deny it to everyone.

The primary reason why communism invariably brings poverty is that it is a mendacious ideology, whose unexpressed purpose is subjecting individuals. The second reason, which is one of the ways in which that purpose is realized, is that it violates fair exchange and the rules of the production-money relationship: it remunerates non-production and it does not adequately pay actual production.

Those who embrace communism are not necessarily insane. They are often people who desire a just and fair world, being scammed.

China's development is due to the introduction of a market economy and private enterprise since the 1970s. It is a hybrid system where some capitalist excesses are harnessed by a vigorous government that does not allow private interests to overcome state interests. The legacy of communism is limitations on individual freedoms, indoctrination, media control, and the violent repression of minorities.

CHANGE

Man is not used to *change*. His spiritual nature transcends time, its key ingredient. Change is movement, by nature it conflicts with the static nature of the Self.

Seventy years of peace, indirect democracies, and affluence make the West look like a war-, tyranny-, and poverty-proof haven to the naive eyes of those who do not conceive of change. In fact, they equal the average human life expectancy, so that only one generation could be said to have started and ended their existence in relative comfort.

In this Universe, change is constant. Preservation of the *status quo* is an illusion. Change is produced by the most active, the others are just subject to it.

The *direction* of change depends on *you*.

One day, the World will belong to the honest. Its condition will depend on the sense of urgency individuals derive from the current situation and on the dedication to the Purpose. Will it be an Eden inhabited by a large, thriving, and advanced society, or a desert planet inhabited by a tribe of survivors?

One may feel alone, unheard, ignored, last, but ideas are more contagious than a virus. Truth, like water, always finds a way through rock.

∵